Legislating Fatness

Discrimination based on body weight is an underestimated and widespread problem. There is not a single national law worldwide that prohibits weight discrimination, but quite a number of laws and policies that reinforce, or at least reflect, the existing socially ubiquitous weight stigma.

This volume focuses on where and how fatness and law intersect, discussing current anti-discrimination protections related to fatness; the ongoing debate around the introduction of new anti-discrimination categories; national and international principles that seem to argue against the introduction of legal protection of fatness; the question whether fatness should be considered a disability; and weight stigma in legal practice. Starting from a fat studies perspective, this book also considers the legal implications of anti-discrimination legislation for fatness through an intersectional lens, noting how fatness often overlaps with other marginalized identities, including race and ethnicity, gender, and socioeconomic status. This book will be of interest to both professional and lay audiences, providing an introduction into the legal aspects of weightism, as well as offering solutions for legislative practice. It will be an invaluable resource for everyone who would like to be more weight-sensitive in their legal work.

The chapters in this book were originally published as a special issue of *Fat Studies: An Interdisciplinary Journal of Body Weight and Society.*

Stephanie von Liebenstein is Founder and Vice President of the German Association against Weight Discrimination (Gesellschaft gegen Gewichtsdiskriminierung e.V.), the largest German fat acceptance organization. She has published and presented extensively on weight discrimination, especially its legal implications. The academic editor, writer, and legal scholar lives in Berlin.

Legislating Fatness

Current Debates in Weight Discrimination, Policy, and Law

Edited by
Stephanie von Liebenstein

Routledge
Taylor & Francis Group
LONDON AND NEW YORK

First published 2023
by Routledge
4 Park Square, Milton Park, Abingdon, Oxon, OX14 4RN

and by Routledge
605 Third Avenue, New York, NY 10158

Routledge is an imprint of the Taylor & Francis Group, an informa business

British Library Cataloguing-in-Publication Data
A catalogue record for this book is available from the British Library

ISBN13: 978-1-032-23036-8 (hbk)
ISBN13: 978-1-032-23037-5 (pbk)
ISBN13: 978-1-003-27533-6 (ebk)

DOI: 10.4324/9781003275336

Typeset in Minion Pro
by codeMantra

Publisher's Note
The publisher accepts responsibility for any inconsistencies that may have arisen during the conversion of this book from journal articles to book chapters, namely the inclusion of journal terminology.

This book is dedicated to Cat Pausé (1979–2022)

Contents

Citation Information

The following chapters were originally published in the journal *Fat Studies*, volume 10, issue 2 (2021). When citing this material, please use the original page numbering for each article, as follows:

Chapter 2
Fighting for a (wide enough) seat at the table: weight stigma in law and policy
Angela Meadows, Sigrún Daníelsdóttir, Daniel Goldberg, and Marquisele Mercedes
Fat Studies, volume 10, issue 2 (2021) pp. 101–124

Chapter 3
The anti-stigma principle and legal protection from fattism
Iyiola Solanke
Fat Studies, volume 10, issue 2 (2021) pp. 125–143

Chapter 4
Failure to Launch: One-Person-One-Fare Airline Policy and the Drawbacks to the Disabled-By-Obesity Legal Argument
Jen Rinaldi, Carla Rice, and Emily Lind
Fat Studies, volume 10, issue 2 (2021) pp. 144–159

Chapter 5
Crossroad between the right to health and the right to be fat
Friedrich Schorb
Fat Studies, volume 10, issue 2 (2021) pp. 160–171

Chapter 6
Weight and the law in New Zealand
Cat Pausé and Kathryn Palmer
Fat Studies, volume 10, issue 2 (2021) pp. 172–183

Notes on Contributors

Sigrún Daníelsdóttir, Division of Public Health, Directorate of Health, Reykjavik, Iceland.

Daniel Goldberg, Center for Bioethics and Humanities, University of Colorado Anschutz Medical Campus, Aurora, USA.

Emily Lind, Gender, Sexuality, and Women's Studies Okanagan College Revelstoke, British Columbia, Canada.

Angela Meadows, Department of Psychology, Western University, London, Canada.

Marquisele Mercedes, Department of Behavioral and Social Sciences, Brown University School of Public Health, Providence, USA.

Kathryn Palmer, Anderson Creagh Lai, Auckland, New Zealand.

Cat Pausé[†], Massey University, New Zealand.

Carla Rice, Re•Vision: The Centre for Art and Social Justice, College of Social & Applied Human Sciences, University of Guelph, Canada.

Jen Rinaldi, Legal Studies, Ontario Tech University, Oshawa, Canada.

Friedrich Schorb, Health and Society, Institute for Public Health and Nursing Research, University of Bremen, Germany.

Iyiola Solanke, Law, University of Leeds, UK.

Stephanie von Liebenstein, Association against Weight Discrimination (Gesellschaft gegen Gewichtsdiskriminierung e.V.), Berlin, Germany.

Fatness, disability, and anti-discrimination law: an introduction to the basic concepts*

Stephanie von Liebenstein

ABSTRACT
In view of increasing attention for the topic of fatness, discrimination, and law, there is a rising international demand for the inclusion of the protection category "weight" in anti-discrimination laws. However, what is often overlooked is the complexity of the juridical debate. The definition of "discrimination", for example, varies in laws internationally, and the effectiveness of anti-discrimination clauses depends strongly on whether they are contained in e.g. criminal law, civil law or constitutional law. This introduction tries to shed light on some of the ambiguities in the debate, in particular whether fatness should be a subset of the discrimination category "disability", taking the social model of disability as a basis. It argues that the social model of disability and its focus on a socio-dynamic definition of disability is very often misunderstood as not requiring an "impairment" to be applicable in the first place. In light of the fact that fat activists have fought the medicalization of fat bodies for decades now, the author makes a case that it would ultimately be inconsistent for fat activists and fat studies scholars to push the concept of fatness as a disability in its own right. The ADA (American with Disabilities Act) "regarded as" prong is also taken into account. – Another light is shed on how intersectionality can be represented legally. The article ends with a suggestion of what an anti-discrimination law protecting fat people should ideally look like, and exemplifies which areas of "fatness and law" might, among others, be worth working on.

Weight discrimination – disadvantageous treatment based on a person's body weight – is a problem that is as widespread as it is unrecognized not only by society, politics, and the media, but also by the overwhelming majority of researchers. Even those who study the social determinants of health or oppression systems within society like racism, sexism, and ableism hardly ever take note of weightism despite its prevalence. Indeed, not only in the US have the numbers of reported weight discrimination risen constantly since at least 1996

* This introduction is an updated, revised and expanded version of my introduction to *Fat Studies. An Interdisciplinary Journal of Body Weight and Society.* Volume 10, 2021 – Issue 2: Fatness and Law (ed. Stephanie von Liebenstein).

(Andreyeva et al. 2008), to the point of being as high as the rates of racial discrimination in the US (Puhl et al. 2008). The situation is similar in many other countries like Denmark (Greve 2008), France (Huggins 2015), Germany (Hilbert 2008), Greece, Iceland, Korea, Portugal, Spain and Sweden (Puhl et al. 2015, with further references). Fat people[1] face weight discrimination in almost all areas of daily life, from bullying in the school yard to negative representation in educational material, from lack of access to institutions of higher education, disadvantages in the job recruitment process and employment settings to de-humanizing representation in the media and in advertisement, stigmatization in health care, access to fitting public accommodations and to suitable consumer goods, especially fashion (Puhl, Heuer 2009). In employment settings, fat people are regularly confronted with a whole plethora of unfair practices in hiring, salary, promotion prospects, and job termination compared to thin colleagues, and also often bullying (Rudolph et al. 2009). In France, 70% of fat people complain about repeated weight discrimination in the public sphere, at school, at work, at home, and even in health care settings (Odoxa 2020). In employment, weight is the one most prevalent ground of discrimination in the very prominent French "physical appearance" category which affects most employment-related discrimination cases (Défenseur des droits 2020).[2] In the UK, fat women are treated particularly unfairly in job settings, facing a wage penalty of several hundred dollars per year for every additional BMI point (Tyrell et al. 2016). In Germany, they are usually not being considered for high-esteem jobs like lawyer and CEO even if they have the necessary qualifications (Giel et al. 2012).

However, there are only few places in the world where there is explicit legal protection against weight discrimination. This includes the state of Michigan and the cities of San Francisco, California; Santa Cruz, California; Washington, D.C., and Binghampton, New York in the USA that number "weight" among their categories protected against discrimination in their municipal codes or (in the state of Michigan) in the Elliott-Larsen Civil Rights Act of 1976.[3] The Icelandic capital Reykjavik, being the first in the world outside the U.S., also has a Human Rights Policy which names "height and weight" directly as protected categories (Art. 6, revised version 2016).[4]

There are a number of places where "physical appearance" or "physical features" is a protected discrimination ground, like France (Code Pénal); Belgium (Loi tendant à lutter contre certaines formes de discrimination); the state of Victoria, Australia (VIC Equal Opportunity Act 2010); Madison, WI, USA (Madison City Code); Urbana, Ill, USA (Urbana Human Rights Ordinance); and Washington, D.C., USA (District of Columbia Human Rights Law). While some of the relevant antidiscrimination agencies (like the Défenseur des droits in France (2016) and the Victorian Equal Opportunity and Human Rights Commission (2021)) explicitly mention weight discrimination as an instance of physical appearance or physical features discrimination, this does not mean that a category named e.g. "physical appearance" has proven particularly effective for fat people so far (von Liebenstein 2021).

Time and again fat activists and scholars of various disciplines have demanded that fat people enjoy legal protection in a similarly explicit manner elsewhere by including "weight" as a protected category in anti-discrimination law. What sometimes gets lost in this important debate, however, is its legal complexity. Often there is a lack of knowledge about the basics of legal protection against discrimination, even of what "discrimination" actually means, which legal fields and issues may be affected when a person is discriminated against because of their weight, and what difference it makes whether an anti-discrimination provision is incorporated into constitutional law, criminal law, private law or civil rights laws. My focus in this article is thus not so much on providing a comprehensive introduction into the topics of fatness and law – I have already done that in my article "Fatness, discrimination & law – An international perspective" in *The Routledge International Handbook of Fat Studies* (von Liebenstein 2021) – but rather to discuss a few terms that help to understand these topics. In addition, I will touch upon some issues that I believe have so far been discussed without full appreciation of their inherent complexity. Topics will be the concept of discrimination in all its forms; weight discrimination and the legal areas in which it may take place; the difference between anti-discrimination clauses in civil law, public law and criminal law; discrimination categories and post-categorical law; the debate about fatness as a disability in its own right; and intersectionality. The lodestar of these very disparate topics will be the question of what has to change for fat people to enjoy effective legal protection against weight discrimination.

When people hear or read about weight discrimination, this usually refers to the employer-employee relationship or about injustices in the recruitment process. Weight discrimination, however, does not just pertain to labor law, but also to many other areas of civil and administrative law. This includes instances when fat people are made to pay for two airline seats, are not being served in restaurants, are denied treatment at the medical practice, are excluded from Boy Scout camp (*Overweight Advocates* 2013), sign a prenuptual agreement declaring that they will not gain any weight (Dewberry v. George 2003), are rejected by a university because of their weight, are not allowed to enter civil service,[5] are excluded from jury duty (People v. Wynn 2004), or cannot get an extension of their work visa because of their weight (*South African chef* 2013). Questions of health insurance law or child and youth welfare law may be affected if fat people are denied health insurance, forced to accept disadvantageous insurance tariffs, or when parents lose custody of their child because of their child's weight. Last but not at all least, weight discrimination can also become criminally relevant when fat people are bullied, insulted or assaulted.

Fat discrimination and law in fat studies literature and beyond

The fact that there is generally no or only inadequate legal protection against weight discrimination has alarmed activists and fat studies scholars for decades. Esther Rothblum, editor of the groundbreaking *The Fat Studies Reader*, pointed out employment discrimination and employment-related victimization as early as 1990 (Rothblum et al. 1990). Ten years later, Sondra Solovay dedicated an entire book (*Tipping the Scales of Justice: Fighting Weight-Based Discrimination*) to weight discrimination and the legal system in which she also discussed the question of whether fat people should have legal protection and whether the existing protected class of "disability" is suitable for fat people to rely on. She covered a wide range of areas from the question of whether parents are legally responsible when a child becomes fat, to medical malpractice, denial of public access, and discriminating public policy.

It was Anna Kirkland who first systematically worked through the legal theory of weight discrimination and who devoted an entire book (2008) on *Fat Rights: Dilemmas of Difference and Personhood*. Her approach is to place weight discrimination in the wider context of the civil rights tradition and to discuss weight as another candidate for a class protected under antidiscrimination law, highlighting the differences and similarities between weight and traditional discrimination classes such as gender, race, and disability. Kirkland is one of the most vocal voices in the debate; she has published extensively on fatness and law from a non-stigmatizing perspective.

Tirosh's (2012) article "The Right to be Fat," in turn, argues not only for protection against discrimination but for the right to be fat as a fundamental right, similar to the right to free speech. She argues that in a country in which a great number of highly personal decisions such as marriage, religion, procreation, and education are domains of rights protected by constitutional law (like most other fat studies scholars, she talks about the USA here), the (fat) body should be a domain of rights as well: as part of personal liberty, autonomy and dignity.

Cooper (1997, 2009, 2016), Herndon (2002, 2021), Harjunen (2004) and Mollow (2015) have, among others, contributed significantly to the debate about whether fatness should be recognized as a disability. Their work will be discussed in the course of this introduction.

Many insights into the legal side of weight discrimination, however, stem from scholars working in what might be termed "Critical Obesity Studies" or even just "Obesity Studies"; that is, they conduct valuable research into the workings of weight discrimination – sometimes employing a "critical" sociological perspective – but are usually embedded into an "obesity prevention and counteraction" background. Their scholarship is highly relevant for those from a fat studies background interested in improving the legal situation of fat people.

Many useful (also international) studies have, for example, been conducted by Rebecca Puhl and her research group (Pomeranz and Puhl 2013; Puhl and Heuer 2011; Puhl et al. 2015) and also Anja Hilbert and Claudia Luck-Sikorski and their stigma research groups (e.g. Spahlholz et al. 2016), although they all work in settings that can be called at least averse to fat acceptance. I am personally of the opinion that there should be more of an exchange between scholars in the fat studies community and those whose work is funded by institutions that support "obesity" prevention and counteraction. While I'm convinced we should by no means tolerate discriminatory terminology or thought, I think research by people for whom fatness is problematic may still be extremely relevant and useful for our own research and activism goals.

Nevertheless, there are still numerous gaps in the debate that can only be filled through further research. In particular, I hope that international lawyers, legal scholars and other legal professionals will be sensitized to the topic and write research that will not only be received by other scholars but that makes the legal mainstream take notice, allowing it to influence judicial decisions.

What is "law", anyway?

In 2009, Charlotte Cooper rightly complained that fat studies were still far too often "Fat American Studies." In order to counter this centeredness on the US this volume takes an international approach. In addition to contributors from the US, voices from New Zealand, UK, Canada, Iceland and Germany have their say. Because of this diversity (still far too small and largely English-language), questions around the basic terms used in this debate arise in a much more complex way than if only one national legal culture were to be scrutinized.

The first question in a law-centered volume must of course be: What is law, anyway? And since the answers to this question can be as varied as the different legal cultures with which we are dealing, a broad understanding of law should be used here, in which "law is a body of rules of action or conduct prescribed by the controlling authority, and having binding legal force" (Black's Law Dictionary (1990), accessed 2020). Law is "that which must be obeyed and followed by citizens subject to sanctions or legal consequence" (Black's Law Dictionary (1990), accessed 2020). In Germany, as a rule, a law must be general and abstract, that is, it must be applicable to a large number of people and a large number of issues. This is probably the case in many other countries, too. In the US and other countries there is sometimes a confusing variety of norms that count as "law," namely statutes, treaties, case law, (administrative agency) regulations, executive orders, and local laws. Law in the US and many other countries is made by federal, state, and local legislatures, judges, the president, state governors, and administrative agencies.

However, this volume also discusses policies and internal guidelines that aren't laws in the strictest sense of the word.

What is discrimination, then?

Next, it is important to clarify what discrimination actually means. According to the sociological definition by Hillmann (1994), discrimination denotes a disadvantage or degradation of groups or individuals according to certain values or due to unreflected, sometimes also unconscious attitudes, prejudices or emotional associations. The sociological definition thus includes on the one hand active, willful acts, but on the other hand also mere attitudes that may not necessarily express themselves in deliberate acts, but can represent a reflex reaction to an internalized social stigma. Privileged treatment of a person, though, is not included in this definition. The Cambridge Dictionary, (accessed 2020), in turn, defines discrimination as "treating a person or particular group of people *differently* [italics not in original text], especially in a worse way from the way in which you treat other people, because of their skin color, sex, sexuality, etc." Here the word "discrimination" is understood more literally in the original sense of "to discriminate or to differentiate between X and Y" and includes both disadvantages and advantages.

Indeed, discrimination is understood differently in the various laws internationally, namely on the one hand as an unjustified *disadvantage* based on a category protected by law or, more generally, as an unjustified *differentiation* based on a category protected by law. If the latter definition is used as a basis, a criterion is additionally required to determine which of the differentiations is disadvantageous.

The European Court of Justice (ECJ) has defined discrimination for over forty years as the "application of different rules to comparable situations or the application of the same rule to different situations" (Tobler 2005; Wentholt 1999; De Vos 2007). As a matter of fact, and as Minow (1990) shows in her seminal work *Making all the Difference*, discrimination is not only caused by unequal treatment, but sometimes also by equal treatment. Depending on whether different characteristics such as gender, race or disability need to be ignored or taken into account in order to "level the playing field," equality or equity – sometimes called "equality of chances" – are needed. Where fatness is concerned, in many cases it would be already helpful if it were simply ignored (that is, equality would suffice); in some cases, however, inequality is needed to achieve equality (that is, equity is needed). In the work environment, for example, someone might need a more stable and wider office chair than their thin colleagues, a deeper driver's cab in the delivery van, or other adapted equipment to create equality between fat and thin employees. Equality as a goal therefore requires, on the one hand, *refraining* from treating people differently, and on the other hand *positive action*, for example adaptation of the work environment so that it is suitable for a fat person.

It is important to note that discrimination in jurisprudence is often defined as unequal treatment that occurs *without a justifiable objective reason.*[6] Thus, in many countries not every form of differentiation is relevant to law: Discrimination in the legal sense often needs a discrimination ground specified in the relevant code *plus the absence of a justifying objective reason* (meaning the discrimination is not, as the British Equality Act 2010 phrases it in e.g. sect. 13 (2), a "proportionate means of achieving a legitimate aim").

Direct/indirect discrimination

Another important distinction to bear in mind is that between direct and indirect discrimination. Direct discrimination occurs when a person is disadvantaged relative to another person because of their belonging to one of the protected categories mentioned in the relevant code (Equality and Human Rights Commission 2019). Examples would include a Black person not hired because of their skin color or a person with a disability turned away at the door of a discotheque. On the other hand, discrimination is indirect when the differentiation criterion is not directly linked to a discrimination feature but to criteria that are typically closely related to a legally protected feature (Equality and Human Rights Commission 2019). As a rule, these are apparently neutral regulations, criteria or procedures which, in terms of their actual effect, put people at a particular disadvantage compared to other people. If, for example, a certain minimum height is required for a position without objective justification, this typically disadvantages women – who are on average shorter than men. If a language test in the national language is required in an application process without the national language being required for the position in question, people with an immigration background are indirectly disadvantaged as they typically have a poorer command of the national language than native applicants.

The importance of discrimination categories

The points made above already show that key to legal discrimination protection is to be discriminated against on the basis of a characteristic protected by antidiscrimination law (or, in some cases, for example US disability antidiscrimination law (ADA as amended by ADAA 2008, Sec. 3 (3)), to at least be *regarded* to have that characteristic). Unfortunately, fat people do not have protection from weight discrimination almost anywhere on earth, because fatness is almost nowhere a protected category under the law. What qualifies as a protected category and why is, unfortunately, only rarely decided by the use of an abstract set of criteria but instead because categories have evolved historically. However, there are voices who try to find abstract criteria, not only for existing categories but also for the inclusion of fatness. Iyiola Solanke, for example, employs her anti-stigma principle to a discussion of weight discrimination in this volume. Kirkland (2008) and Tirosh (2012) took similar approaches, albeit employing different rationales.

If a discrimination feature is not explicitly included in the legal code, one still has the option – at least theoretically, but unfortunately rarely practically (von Liebenstein 2021) – to try and subsume the discrimination characteristic under existing discrimination categories. Subsumption, denoting the application of a life fact to law, is a process functioning very roughly like an umbrella term that comprises various individual terms: In view of the fact that the protected discrimination category "disability" exists in many countries, a relatively extensive debate has arisen about whether fat persons – and if so, starting from which degree of fatness – could be considered disabled without asking for further prerequisites. In Washington D.C., "obesity" is a disability in the context of antidiscrimination law since 2019, which marks another, albeit controversial, milestone in the history of protection against discrimination for fat people (Taylor v. Burlington Northern Railroad Holdings Inc 2019).

In some countries there exist discrimination categories that theoretically have the potential to include weight discrimination, for example "physical appearance" or "status of health," or there are open lists with formulations such as "any other ground," "in particular," "other status," or "a status such as." As discussed in von Liebenstein (2021), these categories have so far proven largely ineffective in protecting fat people from discrimination. There are several reasons for this. More often than not, courts find rationales that prevent fat people from being subsumed under the respective category (e.g. arguing that "physical appearance" only refers to immutable characteristics[7] and that fatness is mutable,[8] or that fat people lack "group" status because they mix with thin people in society, so fatness discrimination is not a result of group conflicts (Wang 2008)).

Also, the chances of success for discrimination lawsuits across all discrimination criteria are generally extremely slim. In the US Federal court, for example, employment discrimination plaintiffs fare worse at every step of the adjudication process than all other litigants (Clermont and Schwab 2004). They are more likely to lose at the pretrial level, are less likely to settle their claims, and thus are more likely to go to trial. At trial, employment discrimination plaintiffs lose disproportionately more often, and when appealing an adverse trial outcome, they do far worse than the respective defendants. Moreover, fat people rarely defend themselves against discrimination. For example, they may be ashamed of their weight, or consider it their private problem for which they are solely responsible (Antidiskriminierungsstelle des Bundes 2016). The practice in some countries of naming court decisions after the plaintiffs (e.g. "Kramer v. Kramer") may also contribute to the fact that stigmatized people do not have the self-confidence to appear before a court that probably will not protect but only further stigmatize them.

Anti-discrimination provisions and their contexts

The attentive reader will already have noticed that I am running the risk of lumping things together that should not be painted with such a broad brush.

When discussing antidiscrimination law with an international scope, categories that do not belong together are too often commingled. When looking at anti-discrimination provisions in various different countries, they can be found in completely different places, with different consequences.

Belgium, Finland, France, Luxembourg, and Spain (this is only by way of example) have enacted **criminal prohibitions** against discrimination.[9] Their violation results in the state sanctioning the penalized behavior. According to the general doctrine of criminal law, the commitment of a criminal offense presupposes the fulfillment of the subjective elements of the offense; that is, as a rule, and probably in most countries, intent or negligence. But if there is unintentional discrimination and no specified further legal responsibility – if, for example, there are no suitable seats for a fat person in a doctor's office or the airplane aisle is too narrow for a fat person to pass through – the criminal law would not apply even if fatness was in fact included as a prohibited ground in antidiscrimination law.[10] Due to the difficulties to prove intent or negligence and the fact that criminal sanctions are *ultima ratio* measures in a constitutional state it may very well be assumed that criminal antidiscrimination provisions are only rarely applied in practice (Degener 2005).

Another place where anti-discrimination clauses are often found is in constitutional law. **Constitutional prohibitions** on discrimination have been issued, for example, by Austria, Brazil, Canada, Gambia, Ghana, Germany, Fiji, Finland, Malawi, New Zealand, South Africa, Switzerland, Uganda, and many other countries (Degener 2005). Compared to criminal law, constitutional prohibitions of discrimination seem to have a much greater steering effect, first because in most states they are high-ranking norms that take precedence over opposing simple laws and other legal norms. Second, constitutional norms are binding for case law and have the potential to lead to legal reforms. Third, constitutional norms receive far more public attention than changes to simple laws. The public debates that go hand in hand with the adoption of anti-discrimination laws are a part of the societal transformation intended and should not be underestimated.

Nonetheless, constitutional anti-discrimination law also has disadvantages that should not be underestimated and that render it largely unproductive for the uses of an individual person affected by discrimination. On the one hand, not all constitutional laws are designed as rights – or subjective rights, as readers from a Continental European background would phrase it (Campbell 2017).[11] That is, they do not necessarily provide individuals with a legally recognized and valid claim to a certain legal object. Second, constitutional norms usually only have direct effect in public law, because they primarily protect against state encroachments. Admittedly, some form of protection against anti-"obesity" state campaigns, for instance, would be very welcome, but to a fat person who lost their job in a private company because of weight discrimination, public law will usually (and again this means in most countries) be of no use. Third, constitutional norms are often deliberately kept vague and general because they are intended to be valid for a large number of cases and over time (Degener 2005). Constitutional norms therefore need interpretation by case law and jurisprudence, which in turn are strongly influenced by the culture of the respective country.

The majority of countries in the world have enacted private or public civil rights laws[12] (Degener 2005). As a rule, these also cover discrimination under labor law; however, the protection areas are very different and cannot be easily compared with one another. Compared to criminal and constitutional anti- discrimination norms, civil rights laws (that can be set in civil or public law) are more detailed and comprehensive in terms of content. More areas of everyday life are covered, and there are usually also special requirements for implementing the prohibition of discrimination. Civil rights anti-discrimination norms usually provide persons discriminated against with a (subjective) right of action between individual citizens or private parties (such as individual v. employer or individual v. company).

The situation becomes even more complicated by the fact that anti-discrimination rights are embedded in different economic and cultural contexts in the individual countries. In Germany, for example, employees stay with the same company for an average of 10.4 years (European Labor Force Survey 2014), while employee tenure in the USA is only 4.2 years on average (US Bureau of Labor Statistics 2018). In consequence, it is at least debatable whether in the US greater value will have to be attached to the fairness of job recruitment procedures whereas in Germany, efficient dismissal protection for fat people will be a more urgent concern.

So, anti-discrimination law does not necessarily equal anti-discrimination law in its effects. The respective contexts must always be taken into account.

Are fat people disabled? On the debate around ableism, fatness and discrimination

When discussing discrimination protection for fat people, it often seems that all problems would be solved if fatness were simply recognized as a sub-set of the discrimination category "disability." That the fat rights movement might profit from joining forces with the disability rights movement with respect to anti-discrimination protection is suggested time and again by various authors, who argue that fat people deprive themselves of political influence when they separate their cause from the causes of the disability rights movement (e.g. Cooper 1997; Harjunen 2004; Herndon 2002, 2021). These authors also reference the fact that society is still far too inclined to base its understanding of disability on the medical model and to fall into the trap of healthism and ableism (e.g. Cooper 1997; Harjunen 2004; Mollow 2015).

Internationally, anti-discrimination rights for disabled people have not existed for that long. In the US, which was a pioneer in this respect and 20 years ahead of global development, these rights have existed for almost

50 years (see the anti-discrimination clauses in the Rehabilitation Act 1973). But in Germany, for example, they have existed only since 1994 when the equality article of the Basic Law (Grundgesetz Art. 3 Para. 3) was supplemented by the sentence "Nobody may be disadvantaged because of their disability" (Degener 2005). US equality law for the disabled – particularly the Americans with Disabilities Act (ADA) of 1990 – served as a model for many of the subsequent reform laws in other countries. The Convention on the Rights of Persons with Disabilities, CRPD, which was adopted by the General Assembly of the United Nations in 2006 and came into force in 2008, was joined by 160 countries by 2015 (German Society for the United Nations, n.d. accessed 2020). The convention prohibits any form of discrimination against people with disabilities. It grants them the same human rights as all other people and specifies these according to possible special needs in order to enable them to live as independently as possible in dignity as part of society.

The convention is based on the social model of disability and defines disability in Art. 1 para. 2 as follows: "Persons with disabilities include those who have long-term physical, mental, intellectual or sensory impairments which in interaction with various barriers may hinder their full and effective participation in society on an equal basis with others." The core element of this conception of disability is the recognition that the marginal position of disabled people in society is not a logical consequence of their health problems, but a consequence of political decisions and individual behaviors based on false assumptions about disability. It is not disabled people that need to be changed, but society and the environment that should no longer disable people. The social model of disability (often also called the socio-dynamic or human rights model of disability) is the subject of disability studies[13] and the basis for the disability rights movement. However, it is no longer entirely undisputed (Shakespeare 2010). The social model shifts the focus from an allegedly individual problem to the ways in which society deals with difference. In contrast, the medical model ties disability to the impairment of the individual person and declares disability to be their individual problem. This model is based on the conviction that disabled people are fundamentally incapable of meeting social demands in their work and private life. Disabled people are not viewed as citizens, but as objects of (state) social policy, recipients of welfare benefits or wards under guardianship and care law (Degener 2005).

The social model of disability – four decades after the publication of the groundbreaking work by Oliver (1983) – is now the basis of the anti-discrimination legislation of 160 countries around the world. Nevertheless, in everyday life and even in court, disabled people are often treated as if they were deficient and, because of their shortcomings, needed special treatment. In addition, there is still a significant stigma attached to the term "disability" as used by mainstream society. Disabled people are still far too rarely seen as a welcome part of a broad spectrum of what it means to be human. Mostly, they are still excluded, otherized and made into a foil against which the "healthy" self can shine all the more radiantly.

This ableism (Campbell 2009) has been increasingly criticized at least since the turn of the millennium, and rightly so. Scholars have started to point out that even fat activists are in fact very much ableist when they indignantly point out that they are definitely not disabled.[14] Charlotte Cooper reflected on this as early as 1997 in her essay "Can a fat woman call herself disabled?" and qualified her fatness as an "impairment" in the sense of the above socio-dynamic definition of disability. She – being one of the very few authors who even acknowledge that the social model of disability needs an "impairment" to be applicable in the first place – uses the term "impairment" "without value judgment as signifying part of our bodies that are physically different to the majority of people in a culture" (39). By making "medicalization" a necessary prerequisite for her definition of "impairment", she avoids including groups such as people of color in this definition.

Unfortunately, her concept runs into a number of problems that even she senses herself when she admits that she has the "gnawing" feeling that she, after all, doesn't really belong to the group of those who can call themselves "disabled" (40). First of all, her definition of "impairment" relies on physical differences from the "majority of people in a culture" (39). Many people who are discriminated against because of their weight and who go to court for this reason, however, are not physically different from the majority of people in their country; think of the applicant for a position as managing director of a Lyme disease and Tick-borne Encephalitis association in Darmstadt, Germany, who was not hired due to weight concerns. She had a completely average BMI of 28.7[15] and, unfortunately, did not stand a chance in court. Or of the Abercrombie & Fitch applicants who were rejected because they were thin but did not conform to model measurements (*Abercrombie & Fitch faces French inquiry over 'models'* 2013). Or of the average size Russian Aeroflot female flight attendants who were disadvantaged because of their weight (*Russia's Aeroflot airline accused of 'sex discrimination'* 2017; Strochlic 2015).

On the other hand, Cooper does not make it sufficiently clear why fat people should, after decades of fighting against "but health" arguments, accept a medicalizing discourse imposed on their bodies; a discourse that turns their bodies into an abnormality in need of rehabilitation. I agree with her that the talk of "impairment" includes a deviation from a body that is considered ideal and "healthy". "Impairment", like "disease" refers to a platonic image of man whose body is a replica of the ideal form, deviations from which are already diseased, different and therefore undesirable. Concepts of illness, disease and impairment are always mediated by social constructions and discourses: There is no bodily state that can safely and naturalistically be considered "diseased" or "impaired."

Thus, remembering the socio-dynamic definition of "disability" from above, there is only very little leeway left for a naturalistic approach to the concept of disability. Social constructs, society and its workings enter at two points of the definition: Once at "interaction with various barriers" that "may hinder [disabled persons'] full and effective participation in society on an equal basis with others", and second at the concept of "impairment."

Indeed, fat people are usually constructed in precisely this manner by a large part of society, so that even if subjectively completely healthy and fit, a disease, impairment or at least a negative physical condition is almost always ascribed to them. But does that, in turn, mean that fat people fit the socio-dynamic definition of disability? The social model of disability, pointing out that disabled people are not disabled by their impairments but by society, still needs an impairment as a prerequisite and reference point. Fat activists and fat studies scholars, however, have argued for decades – in fact, since the very first beginnings of the movement in the 1960s (think of the *Fat underground*) – that fatness in itself is not a disease. We have very good reason and very good arguments to defy medicalization, not to consider ourselves as diseased or impaired, and it remains unclear why we should suddenly and voluntarily adopt the medicalized discourses imposed on our bodies. However, fatness without further impairment does not fulfill the prerequisite for the application of the social model of disability.

Let us consider for a moment a medically healthy plaintiff who is not fat but suffers from stigmatization and social exclusion due to their body being socially constructed as different and thus inferior in other ways. Persons who are read as Black, for example, suffer extreme stigmatization and discrimination in predominantly White societies. However, at least I am not aware of a single legal case anywhere in the world in which a healthy Black person was qualified as being disabled before court, not even in the widest sense of the word, precisely because being Black is not considered a disease or impairment and does not stem from one.

But what about the German case of woman who had been entirely bald from her 13th birthday onwards due to an underlying illness. She sued her health insurance company because they had stopped paying for the custom-made wig for which she needed a yearly replacement (BSG 23.7.2002, B 3 KR 66/01 R). The court argued that – although she did not suffer from a functional impairment – she qualified legally as being disabled because her "participation in social life [was] impaired": "Although [the disease is] not leading to loss or disruption of a motor or intellectual function" it has a "disfiguring effect in women" and makes it "difficult or even impossible for a woman to move freely and at ease among other people", the court argued. As a consequence, "the person concerned withdraws from life in the community and is at risk of becoming lonely". This sounds very much like what fat people experience on a daily basis. It is very doubtful, though, that the court would have considered the baldness of the plaintiff a disability *had it not been the result of an underlying disease*; just like courts usually don't consider fatness a disability if it isn't the result of an underlying disease.

Thus, the question fat people need to ask themselves is whether they are as of now willing to be constructed as "diseased"/"impaired" or not, with all social consequences; precisely because even the most "socio-dynamic" of social models of disability requires an impairment to be applicable in the first place.

Cooper, pondering the question whether she as a fat woman is disabled, is, of course, aware of that problem. To solve it, she invokes Gifford's et al. (1995) concept of the "survivor" (of the mental health system). Indeed, Gifford – albeit, I think, not convincingly – denies the impairment aspect of "disability" to be a necessary prerequisite for "survivors'" identities as disabled. The concept of disability raises some hard and interesting questions in connection with mentally disabled persons, indeed. To macerate the social model of disability up to this point, however, might raise additional demarcation problems that may turn out to be impossible to solve.

Please note that by all this I do, of course, not mean a fat person discriminated against and trying to get compensation before court should not invoke "disability" when making their case. As Marilyn Wann phrases it: "In the dark times you use whatever you have" (cited in Kirkland 2008). If there is a chance the court might award damages for disability discrimination, fat people should by all means use that route. When it comes to political claims, however, for fat people to declare themselves disabled (and thus impaired – even in the most constructionist sense of the word) might not be the most consistent path to tread.

Fatness as a disability under the ADA(A) "regarded as" prong (US)

Recently April Herndon (2021), citing Anna Kirkland (2006), recollected the question whether at least in the US, there might be a chance that fatness qualify as a disability under the Americans with disabilities Act ADA (1990) – and the ADA as amended by the ADA amendments Act (ADAA 2008) – under the "regarded as" prong (sect. III (2) (C) in the old version, 1990). In the US, not only disabled people are legally protected against discrimination on the grounds of disability but also people who are "regarded as having [such] an impairment" (sec. 12102 (1) (C) in the new version, 2008). Since the law's introduction in 1990, law scholars, among them Martha Minow (1997), have applauded the prong as particularly useful for pointing out social stigmata in connection with disability. Kirkland (2006) discusses whether in the US, fatness might be one of those categories that have the potential to be protected under the "regarded as" prong. The argument she sets out from roughly follows the line that although a fat person does not have an impairment they are perceived as having an impairment by a stigmatizing mainstream society and thus fall under the respective "regarded as" prong in ADA (1990) sect. III (2) (C) (now as amended by ADAA (2008) sec. 12102 (1) (C), sec. 12102 (3)). She dismisses the idea, however, as not being useful for fat people as ADA individualizes fatness instead of being helpful in forming a collective, political identity for them (Kirkland 2006).

The argumentation that the "regarded as" prong might prove useful for fat people, however, founders at a much simpler point: The impairment the person protected by ADA(A) is "regarded as" having must be an *actual impairment recognized by law* (Richardson v. Chicago Transit Authority, No. 18–2199 (7th Cir. 2019)). The prong does not cover physical states that are mistakenly interpreted as being an impairment; it merely protects persons *who do not have an officially recognized impairment in the current moment* from discrimination on the grounds of an *officially recognized impairment they only allegedly have.* Fatness, however, is not an officially recognized impairment under US federal law if it is not a result of an underlying physiological disorder (Richardson v. Chicago Transit Authority 2019).

In fact, I am not aware of any US case law past or present in which a fat person was successful before court invoking "regarded as" disability discrimination under ADA(A). The most often-quoted, allegedly "successful" case before the introduction of ADAA is EEOC v. Texas Bus Lines, 923 F. Supp. 965 (S.D. Tex. 1996). Arazella Manuel, a fat applicant for a bus driving position, was rejected by Texas bus lines due to the company medical examiner describing her as unable to get up quickly from her seat and having a "waddling" walking style. The impairment Ms. Manuel was perceived as having, however, was not – as is often wrongly cited – her fatness but the mobility issues she was perceived as having. Thus her success in court did not rely on her fatness being regarded as an impairment but on her *walking style being regarded as a symptom of a mobility impairment.*

So far, at least, the "regarded as" prong has not proven helpful in providing legal discrimination protection for fat people.

Disability without "impairment"?

Most of the world's courts refuse to consider "obesity" without further health conditions a disability – with the exception of those in Washington D.C. that accept "obesity" in and of itself as a disability since 2019 (Taylor Burlington Northern Railroad Holdings Inc 2019). Even the famous case of the fat Danish childminder Kaltoft (Fag og Arbejde (FOA), ECJ (European Court of Justice) 2014) that influenced the jurisprudence of many countries from Australia to India to Hong Kong and is discussed in several articles in this volume, failed because he was too healthy to be considered disabled.

The emphasis of the socio-dynamic definition of disability can, however, be variably set on the social interaction component ("interaction with various barriers . . . ") or the "impairment" component so that in fact there may be social models that are more socio-dynamic than others. This is mirrored in what happens at courts worldwide: In Germany, for example, an employee suffering from a symptomless HIV infection was classified by the labor court as "disabled" because of the stigma surrounding HIV (BAG 2013, December 19–6 AZR 190/ 12; Pärli and Naguib 2012). The Supreme Court of Canada set a particularly strong focus on the socio-dynamic aspect of the social model when it ruled in the landmark human rights case Québec v. Boisbriand: "Disability is more than a biomedical condition and can exist outside of functional limitations [. . .] 'Handicap' may be the result of a physical limitation, an ailment, *a social construct*, a perceived limitation, or a combination of all these factors. [. . .]." (Ontario Human Rights Commission, n.d. accessed 2020).[16] Still, in the HIV case above the employee was diagnosed with a recognized disease; and even the Supreme Court of Canada does not do without the "impairment" component when it says "indeed, it is the *combined effect of all these circumstances* that determines whether the individual has a 'handicap' [. . .]." (Ontario Human Rights Commission, n.d. accessed 2020). In sum: There is no social model of disability that is applicable without an "impairment".

"Disability", in sum, is not a suitable legal category to protect fat people against weight discrimination, at least if one refuses to dilute the social model of disability to a point where it becomes entirely meaningless.

In the US, anyway, social acceptance to regard "obesity" as a disability has so far been lower than support to add weight as a protected class in Civil Rights statutes (Suh et al. 2014).

Intersectionality

There is broad consensus that there is an urgent need for a legal answer to the fact that identities overlap (e.g. "Black" and "fat") and that individually existing discrimination features are often not very helpful in protecting people from discrimination. "Intersectionality" is the keyword that is currently being worked on intensively in many disciplines internationally. However, there is often a lack of clarity about what intersectionality means, especially in a legal context, and about whether it is even allowed to describe overlapping identities without the dimension "Blackness" as intersectional. The concept of intersectionality was developed in 1989 by Kimberlé Crenshaw in a legal context. At the time, Crenshaw only applied it to the intersection of "Black" and "female" but now recognizes that it has the potential to be applied to all possible overlaps (Carbado, Crenshaw, and Tomlinson 2013). It has since become productive in different disciplines and different contexts.

Intersectionality in the legal sense does not, however, encompass every form of overlapping of identities. Crenshaw herself illustrates this employing the case of DeGraffenreid v. General Motors.[17] General Motors fired Black women *en masse* in the late 1970s, but was not convicted of discrimination by the court because neither White women nor Black men were dismissed, so the discrimination in question did not fall either under the category of gender or racial discrimination. As it turned out, the intersection of "female + Black" formed a discrimination category of its own as do other categories in similar situations. If, however, a gay atheist couple intends to rent an apartment, but the landlord is disinclined to rent it to either homosexuals or atheists, the result is not intersectional discrimination, since both the discrimination category "gender" and, depending on the country, "sexual orientation" as well as "religion" or "world view" take effect. Thus, the case of the gay atheist couple is *multiple* (additive) discrimination; in the case of the Black women at General Motors the discrimination is *intersectional*. Note that when intersectional discrimination is concerned, *none* of the discrimination categories in question apply, while in the case of multiple discrimination, *all of them* apply. More on this can be found in Solanke's article in this volume.

There are various approaches for how the problem of intersectionality can be dealt with in a legal context. Many attempts to incorporate intersectionality into law, however, address multiple discrimination and not necessarily intersectional discrimination in the strict sense. For example, the UK plans to introduce a paragraph into its Equality Act (2010) beginning with: "A person (A) discriminates against another (B) if, because of a combination of two relevant protected characteristics, A treats B less favorably than A treats or would treat a person who does not share either of those characteristics" (Equality Act 2010, prospective para. 14). The Australian 2012 Human Rights and Antidiscrimination Bill – that did not come into effect – also aimed to end additive discrimination based on "a particular protected attribute, or a particular combination of 2 or more protected attributes" (Parliament of Australia 2013).

A much more efficient albeit still theoretical approach is the attempt at a post-categorical anti-discrimination law (Liebscher et al. 2012). The concept of intersectionality has in fact been criticized for homogenizing experiences of discrimination, for defining categories in a quasi-essentialist manner, for excluding othered persons and thus ultimately for creating more problems than it solves (Lembke and Liebscher 2014). This is what post-categorical anti-discrimination law tries to resolve by focusing on the experience of being discriminated against rather than on characteristics of disadvantaged people. As a result, even post-categorical anti-discrimination law uses categories; however, they are no longer understood as qualities of disadvantaged people but as results of stigma (cp. Solanke in this volume) and discrimination.

What should anti-discrimination law do?

There remains the question of what an anti-discrimination law that reliably protects fat people from discrimination should be able to achieve. The necessity to enter "weight" or "fatness" or however it might be termed (which is, of course, debatable) into anti-discrimination law as a protected category should be evident now. Ideally, this additional category should be part of a law that grants those who have been discriminated against (subjective) legal rights. The law should also include an intersectional dimension, for example by pointing out that categories are not inherent traits of disadvantaged people but results of social constructions; and that discrimination based on a combination of categories is still legally forbidden discrimination. It must also be ensured that the anti-discrimination law is not only designed as a defensive right but also as a right to positive action or to what is called "affirmative action" in the US in connection with disability law. This might be the only way to ensure that the protection of fat people not only results in not actively disadvantaging them, but also, for example, in providing them with suitably wide office chairs. In addition, a collective right of action and a right of representation is needed – these do not yet exist in all countries.

The article by Angela Meadows, Sigrún Daníelsdóttir, Marquisele Mercedes and Daniel Goldberg in this volume also deals with the question of what would have to change beyond legal anti-discrimination protection considering the fact that weight discrimination pervades legal practice just as much as society as a whole. The law and legal practice are, after all, no more than mirrors of society's values, and distorted ones at that since there usually is a delay of several years before changing values have had the chance to change the law.

A rewarding area of study – and activism

To study the legal side of weight discrimination, like fat studies in general, thus not only opens up the possibility of some exciting scholarly work on a complex and fascinating topic, in a wealth of disciplines and a great variety of legal areas from labor law to social law to criminal, constitutional or youth welfare law (to name just a few), but also the possibility of concrete activism in one's own country. Sigrún Daníelsdóttir was instrumental in influencing the adaptation of the Reykjavik Human Rights Policy in Iceland; Angela Meadows organized the conference that opened the government's eyes. Caitlin Pausé's and Kathryn Palmer's article in this volume offers a draft for a revision of the New Zealand Human Rights Act 1993. And I myself and the German Association against Weight Discrimination have – together with sociologist Friedrich Schorb, who writes about the Right to Health in this volume – been fighting for years to add "weight" as a discrimination category to the German General Equal Treatment Act (the German anti-discrimination law), the Berlin State and Baden-Württemberg Anti-Discrimination Laws.

While "weight discrimination and law" is usually discussed from a perspective of what can be done to change antidiscrimination law, it is also an immensely productive topic where legal practice is concerned (e.g. what do fat people experience when they come in contact with the law; the constructions of fatness in legal practice, etc.). Also, a critical perspective on anti-fat policies may be very enlightening, such as on government "anti-obesity" campaigns, ordinances and programs. It is also rewarding to take a closer look at arguments against adding fatness or "weight" as a protected discrimination ground in anti-discrimination law; for example the claim that it lacks immutability; that fat people are to blame for their weight; that they aren't a "group" and thus cannot be covered by anti-discrimination provisions (Cooper 1997; Wang 2008); or that protection against weight discrimination interferes with the fundamental right to health (see Schorb in this volume). Last but not least it would be immensely instructive to analyze activism aimed at changing the law, including what worked and what didn't. What backgrounds do activists come from, what concept of self, of discrimination and of fatness do they have and what are their primary goals?

I hope that the noticeable positive attitude in the population to protect fat people from discrimination (at least in the area of employment (Puhl et al. 2015)) has consequences, so that legal professionals – internationally – become sensitive to the topic. I hope that that fatness will no longer be considered a medical problem, but a human rights issue, an issue at the core of individual personality, human dignity and freedom. And I hope that in the very near future fat people will be treated as subjects rather than objects of law who have a right to be and to remain fat.

Notes

1. The terms "fat" and "fatness" are employed throughout this volume instead of the more common "overweight" or "obese" as the latter are medicalizing terms suggesting that fatness is a medically problematic state of being in need of therapy and, ultimately, elimination. Fat studies – to which this volume is a contribution – contests this view by pointing out the social constructions around fat bodies and e.g. disease.
2. In France, fatness is the first and foremost immutable ground of discrimination within the "physical appearance" group (Défenseur des droits 2016).
3. Massachusetts has introduced a bill to protect against discrimination on the basis of height and weight in the legislative period 2019/2020, https://www.hsph.harvard.edu/striped/fighting-weight-discrimination-in-massachusetts/. When this article went into press it hadn't been voted on yet (bill S.2495).
4. Also, there are a number of cities and states around the world that subsume "weight" under "physical appearance/features" or "disability" (e.g. Victoria, Australia [VIC Equal Opportunity Act 2010]; Madison, WI, USA [Madison City Code]; Urbana, Ill, USA [Urbana Human Rights Ordinance]; Washington, D.C., USA). More on the pros and contras of subsuming "weight" under other categories see von Liebenstein (2021).
5. This was a serious problem in Germany until 2013 when the Supreme Administrative Court (BVerwG) decided to drop the hurdles for civil service candidates (BVerwG, 2013, October 30 – 2 C 16.12, BVerwG, 2013, December 13 – 2 B 37.13).
6. Cp. e.g. Germany's Allgemeines Gleichbehandlungsgesetz, § 20 and §§ 8–10. The British Equality Act 2010, for example, allows discriminations in certain protected categories if they are "a proportionate means of achieving a legitimate aim" (sect. 13 (2), sect. 15 (1b)).
7. Cp. e.g. Vallor 2013 on a case from 1981 in which an employee of union Pacific was the plaintiff: "obesity was not a disability because it was not an 'immutable condition such as blindness or lameness'".

8. Interestingly, though, the French antidiscrimination body Défenseur des droits has recently begun to consider fatness an immutable feature (Défenseur des droits 2016).
9. Belgium: Loi tendant à lutter contre certaines formes de discrimination, 2007, C–2007/02099. France: Code Pénal, Art. 225-1 to 225-4 CP. Finland: Criminal Code, Sec. 11. Luxembourg: Code Pénal, Art. 454 ff. Spain: Código Penal, 1995, Art. 314.
10. At least in absence of a law regulating aisle or seat widths.
11. The need to add a "subjective" arises in French and German because the terms "le droit" and "das Recht" are terms that can be applied to both law and rights.
12. Namely i.a. Australia, Belgium, Canada, Chile, Costa Rica, England, Ethiopia, Finland, France, Germany, Ghana, Greece, Guatemala, Hong Kong, Hungary, India, Ireland, Israel, Madagascar, Malta, Mauritius, Namibia, Netherlands, Philippines, Portugal, Spain, South Africa, South Korea, Sri Lanka, Sweden, USA, Zambia, and Zimbabwe (Degener 2005).
13. Many people now prefer the term "critical disability studies" (Meekosha and Shuttleworth 2017).
14. While, at the same time, there is also the risk that the label "disabled" is perceived as an appropriation by disabled people who may be in opposition to this kind of colonization of their experiences (Cooper 1997).
15. ArbG Darmstadt (Labour Court Darmstadt, Germany) 2014, June 14 – 6 CA 22/13.
16. The social model of disability articulated by the Supreme Court of Canada has been followed in many Canadian appellate court and Human Rights Tribunal of Ontario (HRTO) decisions and has paved the way for lawsuits related to weight discrimination as disability discrimination, including, but not limited to, the case law following the "One Person, One Fare" policy introduced in 2009 by the Canada Transportation Agency (CTA) for Canadian airlines. For more on this, please refer to the article by Rinaldi and Rice in this volume.
17. DeGraffenreid v. General Motors 558 F.2d 480 and 145 (8th Cir.1977), cited in Crenshaw (1989, 383).

Disclosure statement

No potential conflict of interest was reported by the author.

References

Abercrombie & Fitch faces French inquiry over 'models'. 2013. BBC News, July 25. http://www. bbc.com/news/world-europe-23450486.

Andreyeva T., Rebecca M. Puhl, and K.D. Brownell. 2008. "Changes in perceived weight discrimination among Americans: 1995–1996 through 2004–2006". *Obesity* 2008 (16): 1129–1134.

Antidiskriminierungsstelle des Bundes. 2016. *Evaluation des Allgemeinen Gleichbehandlungsgesetzes.* Berlin: Antidiskriminierungsstelle des Bundes.

Black's Law Dictionary. 1990. "Law." https://thelawdictionary.org/.

Cambridge Dictionary. n.d. "Discrimination." https://dictionary.cambridge.org/de/worter buch/englisch/discrimination.

Campbell, Fiona Kumari. 2009. *Contours of Ableism: The Production of Disability and Abledness.* Basingstoke: Palgrave Macmillan.

Campbell, Kenneth. 2017. "Legal Rights." In *The Stanford Encyclopedia of Philosophy*, edited by Edward N. Zalta. https://plato.stanford.edu/archives/win2017/entries/legal-rights/.

Carbado, Devon W., Kimberlé Crenshaw, and Barbara Tomlinson. 2013. "Intersectionality: Mapping the Movements of a Theory." *Du Bois Review Social Science Research on Race* 10 (2):303–12. doi:10.1017/S1742058X13000349.

Clermont, Kevin M., and Steward J. Schwab. 2004. "How Employment Discrimination Plaintiffs Fare in Federal Court." *Journal of Empirical Legal Studies* 1:429–58. doi:10.1111/ j.1740-1461.2004.00013.x.

Cooper, Charlotte. 1997. "Can a Fat Woman Call Herself Disabled?" *Disability & Society* 12:31–42. doi:10.1080/09687599727443.

Cooper, Charlotte. 2009. "Maybe It Should Be Called Fat American Studies?" In *The Fat Studies Reader*, edited by Esther Rothblum and Sondra Solovay, 327–33. New York: New York University Press.

Cooper, Charlotte. 2016. *Fat Activism. A Radical Social Movement*. Bristol: HammerOn.

Crenshaw, Kimberlé W. 1989. "Demarginalizing the Intersection of Race and Sex: A Black Feminist Critique of Antidiscrimination Doctrine, Feminist Theory and Antiracist Politics." *University of Chicago Legal Forum* 8 (1):139–68.

Défenseur des droits. 2016. *Études & Résultats. 9e édition du barométre du Défenseur des droits et de l'OIT sur les perceptions des discriminations dans L'emploi. „Le physique de l'emploi"*. http://www.cfdt-culture.org/wp/wp-content/uploads/2017/01/DDD_9e_barometre_ defenseur_des_droits_fevrier2016.pdf.

Défenseur des droits. 2020. *13éme barométre. La perception des discriminations dans l'emploi.* https://www.ilo.org/wcmsp5/groups/public/---europe/---ro-geneva/---ilo-paris/documents/publication/wcms_763022.pdf.

De Vos, Marc. 2007. *Beyond Formal Equality – Positive Action under Directives 2000/43/EC and 2000/78/EC*. European Commission Directorate-General for Employment, Social Affairs and Equal Opportunities Unit G.2. https://op.europa.eu/en/publication-detail/-/publica tion/5fc68cca-c88a-4800-bcfd-b8ce17ddab36

Degener, Theresia. 2005. "Antidiskriminierungsrechte für Behinderte: Ein globaler Überblick." *Zeitschrift für ausländisches öffentliches Recht und Völkerrecht* 65:887–935.

Equality and Human Rights Commission of the United Kingdom. 2019. "What Is Direct and Indirect Discrimination?" https://www.equalityhumanrights.com/en/advice-and-guidance/what-direct-and-indirect-discrimination.

European Labor Force Survey. 2014. Quoted in. https://www.spiegel.de/karriere/betriebstreue- so-schnell-wechseln-die-deutschen-ihren-job-a-1158685.html.

German Society for the United Nations. n.d. "Rechte von Menschen mit Behinderung." https://menschenrechte-durchsetzen.dgvn.de/menschenrechte/diskriminierungsschutz/rechte-von-menschen-mit-behinderungen/.

Giel, Katrin E., Stephan Zipfel, Manuela Alizadeh, Norbert, Schäffeler, Carmen Zahn, Daniel Wessel, Friedrich W. Hesse, Syra Thiel, and Ansgar Thiel. 2012. "Stigmatization of obese individuals by human resource professionals: an experimental study". *BMC Public Health* 12: 525.

Gifford, G., Beresford, Peter, and C. Harrison. 1995. "Further Links". *Open Mind: The Mental Health Magazine 78*: 20–21

Greve, Jane. 2008. "Obesity and labor market outcomes in Denmark." Economics & Human Biology 2008 (6/3): 350–362. doi: 10.1016/j.ehb.2008.09.001.

Harjunen, Hannele. 2004. "Exploring Obesity through the Social Model of Disability." In *Gender and Disability Research in the Nordic Countries*, edited by Rannveig Traustadóttir and Kristjana Kristiansen, 305–24. Lund: Studentlitteratur.

Herndon, April. 2002. "Disparate but Disabled Fat Embodiment and Disability Studies." *Feminist Formations* 14 (3):120–37.

Herndon, April. 2021. "Fatness and disability: Law, identity, co-constructions, and future directions." In *The Routledge International Handbook of Fat Studies*, edited by Caitlìn Pausé and Sonya Renée Taylor, 88–100. London: Routledge.

Hilbert, Anja, W. Rief, and Elmar Brähler. 2008. "Stigmatizing attitudes towards obesity in a representative population-based sample: Prevalence and psychosocial determinants". *Obesity* (16): 1529–1534.

Hillmann, Karl-Heinz. 1994. "Diskriminierung." In *Wörterbuch der Soziologie* (= Kröners Taschenausgabe. Band 410), edited by Karl-Heinz Hillmann, 155. Kröner: Stuttgart.

Huggins, Michael L. 2015. “Not “Fit” for Hire: The United States and France on Weight Discrimination in Employment.” *Fordham International Law Journal* (38): 889–952.
Kirkland, Anna. 2008. *Fat Rights: Dilemmas of Difference and Personhood.* New York, London: New York UP.
Lembke, Ulrike, and Doris Liebscher. 2014. “Postkategoriales Antidiskriminierungsrecht? Oder: Wie kommen Konzepte der Intersektionalität in die Rechtsdogmatik?” In *Intersektionelle Benachteiligung und Diskriminierung. Soziale Realitäten und Rechtspraxis*, edited by Veronika Apostolovski, Isabella Meier, Simone Philipp, Karin Maria Schmidlechner, and Klaus Starl, 261–90. Baden-Baden: Nomos.
Liebscher, Doris, Tarek Naguib, Tino Plumecke, and Juana Remus. 2012. “Wege aus der Essentialismusfalle: Überlegungen zu einem postkategorialen Antidiskriminierungsrecht.” *Kritische Justiz* 45 (2):204–18. doi:10.5771/0023-4834-2012-2-204.
Meekosha, Hellen, and Russell Peter Shuttleworth. 2017. “What’s So Critical about Critical Disability Studies?” In *The Disability Studies Reader*, edited by Lennard J. Davis, 175–94. London: Routledge.
Minow, Martha. 1990. *Making All the Difference. Inclusion, Exclusion and American Law.* Ithaca and London: Cornell University Press.
Mollow, Anna. 2015. “Disability Studies Gets Fat.” *Hypatia: A Feminist Journal of Philosophy* 30 (1):199–216. doi:10.1111/hypa.12126.
Odoxa. 2020. *La grossophobie en France. Discriminations et l’obésité: État des lieux.* http://www.odoxa.fr/sondage/discriminations-fleau-francais-plus-particulierement-situation-dobesite/
Oliver, Michael. 1983. *Social Work with Disabled People.* London: Macmillan.
Ontario Human Rights Commission. n.d. “What Is a Disability?” http://www.ohrc.on.ca/en/policy-ableism-and-discrimination-based-disability/2-what-disability#_edn27.
Overweight advocates decry Boy Scout Jamboree policy. 2013. “United Press International.” July 19, https://www.upi.com/Odd_News/2013/07/19/Overweight-advocates-decry-Boy-Scout- Jamboree-policy/UPI-88661374259634/?spt=hs&or=on.
Parliament of Australia. 2013. *Exposure Draft of the Human Rights and Anti-Discrimination Bill 2012.* https://www.aph.gov.au/Parliamentary_Business/Committees/Senate/Legal_and_Constitutional_Affairs/Completed_inquiries/2010-13/antidiscrimination2012/report/index.
Pärli, Kurt, and Tarek Naguib. 2012. *Schutz vor Benachteiligung aufgrund chronischer Krankheit. Die Expertise im Überblick.* Berlin: Antidiskriminierungsstelle des Bundes.
Pomeranz, Jessica, and Rebecca M. Puhl. 2013. “New Developments in the Law for Obesity Discrimination Protection.” *Obesity* 21 (3):469–71. doi:10.1002/oby.20094.
Puhl, Rebecca M., T. Andreyeva, and K.D. Brownell. 2008. “Perceptions of weight discrimination: prevalence and comparison to race and gender discrimination in America”. *International Journal of Obesity* 2008 (32): 992–1000.
Puhl, Rebecca M., and C.A. Heuer. 2009. “The stigma of obesity: A review and update.” *Obesity* 2009 (17): 941–964.
Puhl, Rebecca M., and Chelsea A. Heuer. 2011. “Public Opinion about Laws to Prohibit Weight Discrimination in the United States.” *Obesity* 19 (1): 74–82. doi:10.1038/oby.2010.126.
Puhl, Rebecca M., Janet D. Latner, Kerry O’Brien, Jörg Luedicke, Sigrun Danielsdottir, and Ximena Ramos Salas. 2015. “Potential Policies and Laws to Prohibit Weight Discrimination: Public Views from 4 Countries.” *The Milbank Quarterly* 93 (4):691–731. doi:10.1111/1468-0009.12162.
Rothblum, Esther, Pamela A. Brand, Carol T. Miller, and Helen A. Oetjen. 1990. “The Relationship between Obesity, Employment Discrimination, and Employment-related Victimization.” *Journal of Vocational Behavior* 37: 251–66. doi:10.1016/0001-8791(90) 90044-3.
Rudolph, C.W., C.L. Wells, M.D. Weller, and B.B. Baltes. 2009. “A meta-analysis of empirical studies of weight-based bias in the workplace”. Journal of Vocational Behavior 2009 (74): 1–10.
Russia’s Aeroflot airline accused of ‘sex discrimination’. 2017. BBC News, April 20. http://www.bbc.com/news/world-europe-39653381.
Shakespeare, Tom. 2010. “The Social Model of Disability.” In *The Disability Studies Reader*, edited by Lennard J. Davis, 266–73. New York: Routledge.

Solovay, Sondra. 2000. *Tipping the Scales of Justice: Fighting Weight-based Discrimination.* Amherst, NY: Prometheus Books. Kindle.
South African chef 'too fat' to live in New Zealand. 2013. BBC News, July 27. http://www.bbc.com/news/world-asia-23475583.
Spahlholz, Jenny, Baer, Nadja-Raphaela, König, Hans-Helmut, Riedel-Heller, Steffi, and Luck-Sikorski, Claudia 2016. "Obesity and discrimination - a systematic review and meta-analysis of observational studies". *Obesity Reviews* 17 (1):43–55. doi: 10.1111/obr.12343.
Strochlic, Nina. 2015, September 15. "Airline Grounds 125 Flight Attendants for Being 'Fat'." *The Daily Beast.* https://www.thedailybeast.com/airline-grounds-125-flight-attendants-for-being-fat.
Suh, Young, Rebecca M. Puhl, Sai Liu, and Frances Fleming Milici. 2014. "Support for Laws to Prohibit Weight Discrimination in the United States: Public Attitudes from 2011 to 2013." *Obesity* 22 (8):1872–79. doi:10.1002/oby.20750.
Tirosh, Yofi. 2012. "The Right to Be Fat." *Yale Journal of Health Policy, Law, and Ethics* 12 (2): 264–335.
Tobler, Christa. 2005. *Indirect Discrimination: A Case Study into the Development of the Legal Concept of Indirect Discrimination under EC Law.* Antwerp: Intersentia.
Tyrell, Jessica, Samuel E. Jones, Robin Beaumont, Christina M. Astley, Rebecca Lovell, Hanieh Yaghootkar, Marcus Tuke, Katherine S Ruth, Rachel M. Freathy, Joel N. Hirschhorn, Andrew R. Wood, Anna Murray, Michael N. Weedon, and Timothy M. Frayling. 2016. "Height, body mass index, and socioeconomic status: mendelian randomisation study in UK Biobank." *BMJ* 2016; 352:i582.
US Bureau of Labor Statistics. 2018. "Employee Tenure in 2020." https://www.bls.gov/news. release/pdf/tenure.pdf.
Vallor, J. 2013. "Gut check: Why obesity is not a disability under Tennessee law and how the legislature can address the obesity epidemic". *Tennessee Law and Society* (9/2): 265–326.
Victoria Equal Opportunity & Human Rights Commission. 2021. "Physical features". https://www.humanrights.vic.gov.au/for-individuals/physical-features/.
von Liebenstein, Stephanie. 2021. "Discrimination, Fatness & Law – An International Perspective." In *The Routledge International Handbook of Fat Studies*, edited by Caitlin Pausé and Sonya Renée Taylor, 132–149. London: Routledge.
Wang, Lucy. 2008. „Weight discrimination. One size fits all remedy?" *The Yale Law Journal* 117: 1900–1945. https://core.ac.uk/download/pdf/157778987.pdf.
Wentholt, Klaartje. 1999. "Formal and Substantive Equal Treatment: The Limitations and the Potential of the Legal Concept of Equality." In *Non-Discrimination Law: Comparative Perspectives*, edited by Titia Loenen and Paulo R. Rodrigues, 53–64. The Hague: Kluwer.

Legislation

Allgemeines Gleichbehandlungsgesetz (AGG) (Germany). 2006. https://www.gesetze-im-internet.de/agg/BJNR189710006.html.
Americans with Disabilities Act (ADA). 1990. https://www.gpo.gov/fdsys/pkg/USCODE-2015-title42/pdf/USCODE-2015-title42-chap126.pdf.
Americans with Disabilities Amendments Act (ADAAA). 2008. https://www.eeoc.gov/laws/ statutes/adaaa.cfm.
Code Pénal (France), Art. 225-1. 2001. "Revised 2016." https://www.legifrance.gouv.fr/ a ffichCodeArticle.do?cidTexte=LEGITEXT000006070719&idArticle= LEGIARTI000006417828.
Code Pénal (Luxembourg), Art. 454 ff. 1997. "Revised 2016/2018." http://legilux.public.lu/eli/ etat/leg/code/penal/20200320.
Código Penal (Spain), Art. 314. https://www.boe.es/buscar/act.php?id=BOE-A-1995-25444.
Criminal Code of Finland, Sec. 11. 1995. "English Translation." https://www.finlex.fi/en/laki/kaannokset/1889/en18890039?search%5Btype%5D=pika&search%5Bkieli%5D%5B0%5D=en&search%5Bpika%5D=1995.

District of Columbia Human Rights Law. Subchpt. 1, § 2–1401.01. https://code.dccouncil.us/dc/council/code/titles/2/chapters/14/.
Elliott-Larsen Civil Rights Act. 1976. https://www.michigan.gov/documents/act_453_elliott_larsen_8772_7.pdf.
Equality Act (UK). 2010. https://www.legislation.gov.uk/ukpga/2010/15/part/2/chapter/2/cross-head ing/discrimination.
Grundgesetz (Germany). 1949. https://www.gesetze-im-internet.de/gg/BJNR000010949.html.
Loi tendant à lutter contre certaines formes de discrimination (Belgium). 2007. "C–2007/ 02099." http://www.ejustice.just.fgov.be/cgi_loi/change_lg.pl?language=fr&la=F&cn=2007051035&table_name=loi.
Rehabilitation Act (USA). 1973. https://www2.ed.gov/policy/speced/leg/rehab/rehabilitation-act-of-1973-amended-by-wioa.pdf.
The City of Reyjavik's Human Rights Policy. 2006. "Revised I.a. 2016." http://reykjavik.is/en/city-of-reykjaviks-human-rights-policy#6.%20Body%20build%20and%20type.
UN Convention on the Rights of People with Disabilities (CRPD). 2008. https://www.un.org/ development/desa/disabilities/convention-on-the-rights-of-persons-with-disabilities.html.

Case law

ArbG Darmstadt (Labour Court Darmstadt, Germany). 2014. 6 CA 22/13, June 14. BAG (Federal Labour Court). 2013. 6 AZR 190/12, December 19.
BSG (Federal Social Court, Germany). 2002. B 3 KR 66/01 R, July 23.
BVerfG (Federal Constitutional Court, Germany). 2017. 1 BvR 2019/6, October 10.
BVerwG (Federal Administrative Court, Germany). 2013a. 2 C 16.12, October 30.
BVerwG (Federal Administrative Court, Germany). 2013b. 2 B 37.13, December 13. DeGraffenreid v. General Motors. 1977. 558 F.2d 480 and 145 (8th Cir.1977).
Dewberry v. George. 2003. 62 P.3d 525, 526 (Wash. 2003).
EEOC v. Texas Bus Lines. 1996. 923 F. Supp. 965 (S.D. Tex. 1996).
Fag og Arbejde (FOA), ECJ (European Court of Justice). 2014. C-354/13 FOA, December 18. People v. Wynn. 2004. WL 417221 (Cal. Ct. App. 2004).
Québec v. Boisbriand (City of). 2000. 2000 SCC 27, 1 S.C.R. 665.
Taylor v. Burlington Northern Railroad Holdings Inc. 2019. No. 96335-5.

Fighting for a (wide enough) seat at the table: weight stigma in law and policy

Angela Meadows, Sigrún Daníelsdóttir, Daniel Goldberg, and Marquisele Mercedes

ABSTRACT

Few jurisdictions provide legal protection against discrimination on the basis of weight despite evidence of pervasive inequalities faced by fat individuals in employment, healthcare, education, and other domains. Yet, in the last two decades, advocacy efforts in several countries aimed to remedy this situation have been largely unsuccessful. We present a cross-national conceptual analysis of three significant anti-discrimination developments regarding weight in the United Kingdom, the United States, and Iceland, respectively, to highlight how the creation, implementation, and enforcement of legal and policy mechanisms that prohibit weight discrimination ironically suffer under the very burden of deeply rooted structural stigmas against fatness and fat bodies that such efforts seek to counter. However, drawing on research around policy change in response to other social movements, we conclude that we may be at a time where broad-ranging policy change could become a reality.

Introduction

Weight stigma is prevalent and well documented in practically every domain of daily life, including employment, education, health care, housing, the legal systems, the media, and in interpersonal relationships (Puhl and King 2013). Although higher-weight individuals, therefore, face pervasive inequality across numerous domains, with consequences for their health and wellbeing and life opportunities, very few jurisdictions provide legal protection against this form of discrimination. Yet, in the last two decades, advocacy efforts in several countries aimed at remedying this situation have been largely unsuccessful. The primary claim of this article is that efforts to make weight a protected category under equality and/or antidiscrimination laws ironically suffer under the very burden of stigma that such efforts seek to counter. The basic idea underlying this claim – that laws and policies channel preexisting stigmas –

should be unsurprising to any readers familiar with stigma scholarship arising specifically out of work in public health law (e.g., Burris 2002; Silverman and Wiley 2017) and sociolegal studies. There is overwhelming evidence that law is a potent mediator of stigma, all too frequently acting to intensify social stigmas that are, by virtue of the concept of stigma itself, always directed to more marginalized groups in any given society. However, there is at least some reason for optimism in the recognition that law mediates stigma (Burris 2002); where laws can and are used to intensify such stigma, it also follows that their power can be harnessed to ameliorate preexisting stigma. The ethical imperative for doing so should be obvious: stigma is corrosive, is strongly associated with adverse physical, social, and emotional health outcomes, and contravenes basic mandates of social justice (Goldberg 2017).

While the notion that laws and policies mediate stigma is well settled, this powerful mechanism for inscribing "stigma power" (Link and Phelan 2014) has neither been adequately conceptualized and explored in the context of fat stigma nor completed via analysis of specific anti-fat-discrimination laws and policies in the global North. This article aims to begin filling both of these gaps via a cross-national conceptual analysis of three significant anti-discrimination developments regarding weight in the United Kingdom, the United States, and Iceland, respectively. The analysis shows how efforts to make weight a protected category – unquestionably an anti-stigma intervention – can run up against deeply rooted structural stigmas against fatness and fat bodies in each of these societies. On a more optimistic note, the article reviews several legal developments that reflect a more robust commitment to ameliorating weight stigma via law and policy. These developments, of course, do not demonstrate the absence of prevailing weight stigma in any given society – empirically, we know this to be false (e.g., Brewis, SturtzSreetharan, and Wutich 2018; Puhl et al. 2015a) – but rather illustrate the complex relationship between anti-stigma mechanisms in law and policy and the attitudes, practices, and beliefs regarding weight that circulate in the relevant societies. The article concludes by noting that, while laws and policies can be used to alleviate stigma, the structural nature of stigma in general suggests that changes in stigmatizing attitudes, practices, and beliefs are usually more likely to precede legal change rather than to follow it, making interpersonal and community-level stigma interventions equally important in the road to fat liberation.

Before proceeding to the analysis itself, it is important to note the wide scope of what counts as "laws and policies" specifically in fields of public health law and sociolegal studies. Although colloquially "law" is often thought of in the West exclusively in terms of national statutes or constitutions, in fact the laws and policies that shape population health and its distribution go far beyond highly centralized or nationalized constitutions and legislation. In the US, for example, it is widely recognized that administrative law (i.e., regulations) are constitutive of public health law in general and touch people's lives on an everyday level in ways that statutes and constitutions cannot. Moreover, as the analysis in the article shows, regional and local laws and policies (e.g., state laws or municipal ordinances) can also have a dramatic impact on social programs and interventions intended to improve health outcomes. Finally, even on the hyperlocal level, policies adopted by clinics or provider offices can also shape people's experiences of stigma, both in terms of prevalence and intensity. Therefore, and consistent with norms in public health law and legal epidemiology in particular, this article adopts a wide scope for the legal and policy units of analysis.

It is difficult to contest the argument from history that, at least in most Western contexts, law has been extensively used to reinscribe, perpetuate, and even intensify preexisting stigmas (Goldberg 2017; Schweik 2009). One of the central insights of Link and Phelan's (2001) structural model of stigma is what they refer to as "stigma power." By virtue of the roots of stigma in macrosocial power structures, stigma results in significant social consequences; its power is felt by stigmatized groups across a wide variety of social domains, such as education, labor, health care, etc. Laws and policies are a major variable through which stigma power is enacted on the bodies of stigmatized people. Moreover, the evidence that stigma is an independent social determinant of health – perhaps even a true fundamental cause of disease (Hatzenbuehler, Phelan, and Link 2013) – means that stigma power is embodied in ways that reproduce and intensify unequal exposures, life opportunities, and health outcomes.

Crucial to note is the uneven burden of weight stigma across social groups. Members of multiple marginalized groups can carry particularly high burdens of stigma in a fatphobic society (Kasten 2018; Rice et al. 2020; van Amsterdam 2013). For example, fat women are stigmatized more severely than men, and at lower weights (Hatzenbuehler, Keyes, and Hasin 2009); thus, not only do women experience certain disadvantages in a patriarchal system, but fat women experience compound forms of injustice not encountered by thin women or fat men (Hicken, Lee, and Hing 2018). Black women's experiences with fat stigma are affected by an overlap of systemic anti-Blackness and misogyny that significantly shapes their lived experiences (Crenshaw 1991; Daufin 2020); living at the intersection of these axes of oppression creates quantitatively and qualitatively different experiences of stigmatization from those of fat men or fat White women (Cox 2020; Hill Collins and Bilge 2016; Williams 2017). Further, higher-weight status tends to be more prevalent among some racial and ethnic groups, as well as among individuals with lower socio-economic status (Ailshire & House, 2011; Ciciurkaite and Perry 2018). Thus, weight stigma may also act as a proxy for racism and classism (Evans, Davies, and Rich 2008; Makowski et al. 2019; Strings 2015, 2019). However, given intersectionality's multiplicative, rather than additive, nature, it can be difficult to quantify the specifics of how negative outcomes related to weight stigma are impacted by factors like racism or classism (Keith et al. 2017; Reece 2018). It is critical to understand the expression and magnitude of fatphobia as being conditional on the positionalities of who is being stigmatized.

In the following section, we turn to discussion of three specific efforts to harness the mediatory power of public health laws and policies to ameliorate and lessen the devastating power of weight stigma. As the analysis will show, the irony is that the efforts to remedy weight stigma through legal channels are shaped and ultimately impeded by the very stigmas such efforts seek to address. While this finding is not surprising in its own right, it nevertheless has important implications for general efforts to remedy stigma through public health laws, and of course also for specific efforts to redress weight stigma. Note, the first two case studies include examples of blatant fatphobia and may be distressing to some readers.

Three cross-national case studies of law & policy connected to weight stigma

A. Anatomy of an outcry: Response to the Kaltoft case in the UK

In 2014, the European Court of Justice (ECJ) ruled on an unfair dismissal case brought by a Danish childminder, Karsten Kaltoft, against his employer of 15 years, Billund Local Authority, Denmark (*Karsten Kaltoft v Billund Kommune*, 2014; EU: C-354/13). The reason stated for his dismissal was economic cutbacks; however, Mr. Kaltoft was the only childminder to be terminated. In his suit, Mr. Kaltoft claimed that he was dismissed from his position because of his 25-stone (159 kg) size, despite the fact that he was able to fulfil his job role. Under EU law, weight is not a protected category under anti-discrimination legislation. Thus, the ruling hinged on whether or not high-weight status constituted a disability that would be protected under current legislation, namely the Employment Equality Directive (2000/78/EC), which prohibits employment or occupational discrimination on the grounds of age, disability, religion or belief, and sexual orientation.[1] The ECJ ruled that in situations where a worker's size prevents them from "full and effective participation" in their work life "on an equal basis with other workers," then this would be covered under disability laws. The ECJ was quite clear that "obesity"[2] itself is not a disabling condition per se, but only where size became a salient factor in ability to function within the work environment. Ironically, because Mr. Kaltoft's size did not impair his ability to do his job, this situation was not pertinent, and Kaltoft was unsuccessful in his suit, the case ultimately being decided in favor of the local authority. Rulings of the ECJ are binding in all member nations, and, given the moral panic surrounding the so-called "obesity epidemic" (Campos et al. 2006), the decision attracted a lot of attention in the UK media (at the time of writing, the UK was still a member of the EU).

In the following section, we outline responses to the ruling from two distinct groups who were approached by journalists for statements. We focus on a single piece published on the BBC News website (BBC News 2014). This piece was chosen as it was fairly typical of the coverage at the time. In their analysis, the BBC sought comments from two experts in employment and anti-discrimination legislation, and two spokespeople from "obesity" organizations.[3] Their positions are outlined below, and then dissected more carefully to expose the entrenched stigmatizing attitudes underpinning much of the discourse in response to the ruling.

1.The legal experts:

Audrey Williams is an expert in employment and disability law with a particular interest in discrimination, harassment, bullying, and pay inequality. Speaking to the BBC, she noted that the ECJ ruling would increase awareness among employers of their responsibility toward "obese" employees in the workplace. Employment lawyer Paul Callaghan further made clear that this ruling did not change UK law. Under the existing European Equal Treatment Framework Directive, employers are required to make reasonable adjustments, and workers may not be dismissed because of a disability. Thus, a higher-weight individual who suffers co-morbidities such as depression, diabetes, or joint problems that may be directly linked to their size and that impair their ability to conduct their job in some manner would be protected; however, higher-weight workers who are otherwise in good health and experience no specific impairments are not protected from discrimination on the basis of their weight.

2.The "obesity" organizations

Unlike the comments from the legal experts, those from the "obesity" organizations did not state fact or clarify points of law. Rather they conveyed opinions, and, as such, cannot necessarily be generalized to the position of the industry as a whole. However, again, these comments were fairly typical of non-legal commentary at the time. Jane DeVille Almond, chair of the British Obesity Society (BOS), had this to say to the BBC: "If employers suddenly have to start ensuring that they've got wider seats, larger tables, more parking spaces for people who are obese, I think then we're just making the situation worse." She continued, "[The ruling is] implying that people have no control over the condition, rather than something that can be greatly improved by changing behaviour." The BOS is a charitable organization, whose stated mission is to "change attitudes towards obesity, how its [sic] managed, how we can prevent it, and how society responds." They are committed to making "a difference to people whose lives are plagued by obesity" (although not apparently by ensuring they can sit down at work).

Tam Fry, spokesperson for the National Obesity Forum, at the time another charitable organization, told the BBC that the ruling had "opened a can of worms for UK employers." He added, "They will be required to make adjustments to their furniture and doors and whatever is needed for very large people. I believe it will also cause friction in the workplace between obese people and other workers." The NOF now calls itself an independent professional organization that campaigns for a more interventional approach to "obesity," representing a "group of health professionals and specialists who are sickened by the appalling obesity epidemics in the country . . . " In addition to partnerships with a number of health organizations, they list several diet product companies (LigherLife UK Limited, Slim Fast Foods Ltd, Canderel), pharmaceutical companies (Sanofi-Aventis Ltd, Roche Products Ltd, and GlaxoSmithKline UK Ltd), and manufactures of diagnostic and surgical equipment (Abbott Laboratories, Mantis Surgical Equipment Ltd, Tanita UK Ltd) among their partners.

3. Analysis

The outcry in the media and on social media surrounding this ruling centered on the idea of "obesity" being considered a disability. Historically, "disability" has been understood through the medical model, which positions it as some form of defect that rendered a body "abnormal" or deviant. However, political activism by disability rights campaigners since the 1960s has resulted in an evolution of how "disability" is defined and understood (Barnes 2012). Disability advocates reject the binary of normal and deviant bodies, but rather recognize that human diversity exists on a spectrum, and "disability" arises when physical or social barriers serve to arbitrarily draw a line at some point (or rather, multiple points) along this spectrum, beyond which individuals do not have the same access to systems and opportunities that are available to people on the other side of that line (Kaplan 2000).

Since the 1970s, national, international, and supranational organizations have increasingly enshrined a social model of disability into their policies and legislation (for a history, see Barnes 2012). Under this model, a fat individual would not be inherently "disabled," but, for example, if an employer provided office chairs that were rated up to, say, 200 pounds of weight, a 250-lb worker would be prevented from safely engaging in work activities that were within their capabilities and that would be feasible if a chair rated up to 300 pounds were available. Thus, "disability" is a limitation arising from an interaction between human diversity and a (socially) constructed environment that does not take into account that diversity, and, as such, could reasonably be applied to fat bodies (Herndon 2002; Mollow 2015).

Much current legislation on the topic of disability protections is underpinned by the social model of disability. The ruling of the ECJ in *Kaltoft* and the comments by legal experts were based on this understanding of disability as socially constructed. In contrast, public responses reflected outdated, patronizing, and stigmatizing representations of "the disabled" as hapless but blameless victims of circumstance, beyond their control, to be pitied and granted assistance from their benevolent "betters" – the *deserving* disadvantaged.[4] The comments of the spokespeople for "obesity" organizations in the BBC news article were typical in this regard, rejecting the idea that a fat person could be granted the rights given to "disabled" individuals because of their lack of deservingness, as well as the notion that fat people can be disabled at all.

The concept of deservingness is underpinned by two key constructs – culpability and mutability: whose fault is it and could it be fixed? Both factor strongly in weight stigmatizing attitudes. Individuals who score highly on measures of prejudice and fatphobia also tend to score highly on beliefs that weight is under individual control and is simply a matter of personal choice and effort (Crandall 1994). While the scientific literature belies both the idea that fat people can reliably become and remain thin people through their behaviors, or that weight-focused approaches to health are actually salutogenic (for a review, see Calogero et al. 2019), the fact remains that the controllability of body weight is irrelevant from a legal standpoint, at least in the UK and the EU.

On the question of blame, both EU and UK law are clear – the origin of a disability or impairment is immaterial.[5] People are fat for numerous complex reasons, but even if a person were fat through sheer gluttony – a commonly accepted stereotype – any disability or impairment resulting (or structurally produced) from their body size would be covered. As Advocate General Kokott (2012) stated in her opinion in *HK Danmark* (EU C-335/11 and EU C-337/11),

> To define the scope of the directive by reference to the cause of the disability would be arbitrary and would thus be contrary to the very aim of the directive of giving effect to the principle of equal treatment. (point 32)

For individuals struggling with this notion, consider a different example. Imagine two wheelchair users. One lost mobility due to injuries sustained during military service, the other due to a car accident caused by themselves while driving under the influence of alcohol. Do they both get to use the ramp? Or does the person whose injuries were a result of their drunk driving have to pull themselves up the steps with their hands? Although there may be some who would go to this extreme, for most people, the latter suggestion would seem ridiculous. Both have impaired mobility, and both are protected equally against discrimination under the law. Any contention that this is simply not the same as the case with "obesity," is fatphobia at play, rather than a legal distinction.

Mutability, while related to beliefs about blame in the case of weight, is a separate and, perhaps, thornier issue (see Clarke 2015 for an extensive discussion in the context of US equality and anti-discrimination law). Should a person be protected against discrimination based on a trait that could be changed if they so desired? Even assuming that long-term weight-loss was achievable, or even desirable (see e.g., Calogero et al. 2019; Rothblum 2018, for evidence to the contrary), this argument is not applicable to withholding legal protections against weight discrimination in the UK or EU. As noted above, under EU legislation, discrimination on the basis of race or ethnic origin, sex, age, disability, religion, or belief, and sexual orientation are prohibited in employment contexts, and beyond for race, ethnicity, and sex. In the UK, the Equality Act (2010) prohibits direct and indirect discrimination on the basis of nine protected categories: age, disability, gender reassignment, marriage and civil partnership, pregnancy and maternity, race, religion or belief, sex, and sexual orientation. This list contains some protected categories resulting from personal choices and/or that could be changed if desired, yet the law does not require the individual to change. Further, UK legislators have made clear that immutability is also not a consideration in decisions about equal treatment based on disability. Specifically, if an individual has an impairment that would be potentially "treatable" or "fixable" by medical or surgical intervention, use of a prosthesis, or even a special diet, the impairment is evaluated on its severity in the absence of intervention (Equality Act 2010, c. 15 § 6, sched. 1, point 5). Indeed, the necessity of an intervention, broadly defined, to allow an individual to function fully in their daily activities, including normal work activities, is taken as indicative of the adverse effect the impairment is having on their life (Ibid). Thus, again, presenting fatness as a special case in which higher-weight individuals are required to change their bodies to "deserve" equal treatment is no more than fatphobia at work.

Thus, in the UK, a fat person would be protected against discriminatory treatment on the basis of their weight to the extent that their working environment was constructed in a way that their weight became an impediment to their ability to function fully in their role to the same extent as a thinner person.[6] As noted by the legal experts cited in the BBC article, the ruling in *Kaltoft* in no way changed a UK employer's existing duty of care to their employees under both UK and EU law. The comments of both Ms. DeVille Almond and Mr. Fry, suggesting that employers' accommodation of their fat employees should not be encouraged, were, in fact, contrary to employers' actual legal obligations. However, in the absence of any form of impairment, employees are not protected against weight-based discrimination. In the case of Mr. Kaltoft, his employer would have been perfectly entitled to state overtly that the reason he was the sole childminder being fired as a result of supposed economic cutbacks was that they did not like the look of him. They did not say this, but they could have, with impunity.

B. Weight as a protected category: Michigan antidiscrimination law

Weight discrimination *qua* weight discrimination is not illegal in the U.S. (Pomeranz 2008). Some courts, along with the U.S. Equal Employment Commission (2012), have indicated that to the extent fatness may be construed as a "disability," civil rights protections related to disability may shield a fat person from discrimination. However, as in the UK and EU, this shield flows from disability law and does not make weight itself a category protected from discrimination under federal law.

While there are a variety of potential law and policy approaches to countering stigma, specific antidiscrimination provisions are unquestionably an important approach. The significance of such provisions is not bound to the actual substance or enforcement of any given legal structure; the expressive function of law creates signaling effects that reverberate in a given polity. Thus, for example, even while enforcement of the privacy provisions of the U.S. Health Insurance Portability and Accountability Act ("HIPAA") has been uneven, the existence of the federal framework itself prompted significant changes in social and cultural norms within health-care organizations regarding protections for patient privacy (Wilkes 2014).[7]

There is a single exception to the general lack of protections in state and federal US antidiscrimination law for fat people: the state of Michigan. In 1976, the state implemented the Elliott-Larsen Civil Rights Act ("ELCRA"), which prohibits an employer from refusing to hire or otherwise taking adverse employment action against an individual on the basis of "religion, race, color, national origin, age, sex, height, weight, or marital status" (1976, (1)(a)-(b)). In 2002, Kristen observed that "height and weight" were added to the statute because of the ways in which these features tended to be linked to race/ethnicity and to gender (p. 101). The exact number of weight discrimination cases filed with the state Civil Rights Commission pursuant to the statute is unknown, but there are relatively few published Michigan cases explicitly addressing the weight discrimination provision of ELCRA. While published cases are not equivalent to claims, the paucity of the former gives rise to a reasonable inference that the total number of claims brought based explicitly on the weight discrimination provision is not large (likely in the low hundreds at most).

Moreover, as is common in US antidiscrimination litigation, courts have significant leeway in interpreting and applying statutory language. In *Harris v. Hutcheson (2018*, at *9), an intermediate court of appeals reasoned that the defendant employer's recommendation to the plaintiff that she "get healthy and stay healthy" did not pertain specifically to weight and therefore did not constitute direct evidence of weight discrimination under ELCRA. In *Webb v. Swartz Creek Community Schls. (2001)*, the court ruled that the plaintiff had presented no triable issue of fact regarding the defendant school district's discontinuation of plaintiff's service as a bus driver due to the physical difficulty of accessing the steering wheel. According to the court, the plaintiff, who was "morbidly obese," was removed from her position only because her weight "prevented [her] from driving the school bus safely. There is no evidence that … any … District employee made derogatory remarks about

Webb's weight" (at p. 14). And in the per curiam opinion of *Farino v. Renaissance Club (1999)*the court found that the defendant's noted concern about plaintiff's weight in performance reviews "were not hostile or derogatory and ... are not evidence of a weight-based animus" (p. 7). The court was also unmoved by the evidence that the defendant stated that the plaintiff was "fat and stunk," and concluded that no reasonable finder of fact could have concluded that the defendant acted with discriminatory animus in terminating the plaintiff (p. 8–9). The court, therefore, reversed the holding of the trial court and vacated a jury award of nearly US 276,000. USD

This flexibility of enforcement reinforces the primary claim of our article – that even where formal legal and policy mechanisms exist for countering weight stigma at the structural level, prevailing attitudes, practices, and beliefs regarding fat people may hinder efforts to utilize those mechanisms as either the sword or the shield. Admittedly, the existence of cases in which Michigan courts have ruled against plaintiffs asserting weight discrimination claims under ECLRA does not ipso facto establish that prevailing weight stigmas animated the court's reasoning. Nevertheless, the argument that structural stigma influences judicial decisionmaking is neither novel nor unprecedented; legal scholars have argued, for example, that the judicial emasculation of the Americans with Disabilities Act reflects stigma against disabled people (e.g., Soifer 2003). Similarly, U.S. courts have – very obviously – hardly been immune from the pernicious influence of racial stigma in their decision-making (e.g., *Dred Scott, 1857*; *Korematsu v. United States, 323 U.S. 214 1944*; etc.).[8] When we consider the flexibility of ECLRA enforcement through an intersectional lens, fat people who belong to minoritized groups are, once again, particularly vulnerable against weight discrimination that formal legal protections are supposed to help safeguard against.

Still, despite some U.S. courts' apparent hostility to antidiscrimination litigation, and to ECLRA in particular, there do exist cases in which Michigan courts have upheld or affirmed a plaintiff's claims of weight discrimination (e.g., *Lamoria v. Health Care & Retirement Corp., 1998*; *Ross v. Beaumont Hosp., 1988*). Kristen (2002) concluded that

> [c]ourts interpreting Michigan weight antidiscrimination law have thus developed a jurisprudence that closely tracks [U.S. federal] antidiscrimination law ... Plaintiffs have not always prevailed under the Michigan law but some have been successful. It is likely that similar laws in other states would significantly add legal protection for fat workers (p. 104–105).

Moreover, despite the probable low number of total cases, Adamitis (2000) notes that the weight discrimination provisions of ECLRA have in fact produced both settlements and, perhaps more importantly for policy purposes, "the consequent revision of discriminatory employment policies and standards" (p. 210–211).

C. Weight as a protected category: The Body Respect Movement in Iceland

Iceland is a 103,000 km^2 (64,000 sq mi) island in the North Atlantic Ocean with a population of approximately 350,000 (Statistics Iceland 2019). As with most other countries, Iceland has seen great advancement in human rights and social justice in the past decades. In terms of body respect and equality, however, Iceland is a typical western nation with high levels of media consumption, unrealistic appearance ideals, body image concerns and dieting among youth, and high levels of anti-fat bias (Asgeirsdottir, Ingolfsdottir, and Sigfusdottir 2012; Ingolfsdottir et al. 2014; Puhl et al. 2015a). A cross-national study in 2015 found levels of anti-fat bias in Iceland to be comparable to those reported in the United States, Canada, and Australia, with the same underlying beliefs attributing fatness to lack of willpower and personal responsibility (Puhl et al. 2015b).

Since 2006, "body respect" activists have undertaken numerous public awareness campaigns, blogs, events, and community participation activities in order to counter such views and related social injustice. The first action taken by the Icelandic Association for Body Respect (IABR) on its inception in 2012, was to lobby for the inclusion of weight as a protected category in a new national constitution that was in preparation at the time. This spawned a public debate where views were divided between those supporting the proposal, those regarding it unnecessary, and those regarding it preposterous and irresponsible. Indeed, a nationally representative survey of approximately 1,000 Icelanders found a lack of support for legal reform to counter weight discrimination, despite respondents reporting widespread experiences of unfair treatment and discrimination of themselves and of friends and family members (Danielsdottir and Jonsson 2015). Surprisingly, while the majority of respondents agreed that weight discrimination *should be* illegal, only 37% said they would support the passing of legislation making it illegal, and only 20% supported the inclusion of weight in the national constitution as a protected category (Danielsdottir and Jonsson 2015). At the time of this writing, the success of the effort remains unknown as the constitution is still being revised by parliament with the provision on nondiscrimination not set to be addressed until the 2021–2025 electoral term.

Yet, a very different example of attempts to address weight-related social injustice can be found in inclusion of weight as a protected category in the Reykjavik Human Rights Policy issued in 2016 (City of Reykjavik 2016). This initiative arose as a result of the 3rd Annual International Weight Stigma Conference being held in Reykjavik, the capital city of Iceland, in 2015.[9] As part of its year-long program to celebrate the 100-year anniversary of Icelandic women's suffrage, the City of Reykjavik was a major sponsor of the event and representatives from the city's human rights committee were invited to address the conference. The theme of the conference was "Institutionalized Weightism: How to Challenge Oppressive Systems?" and it was, therefore, natural to examine how the city's institutions addressed weight-related justice. At the time, weight-related oppression was not recognized as a discrimination issue; however, when the absence of "weight" from the city's human rights policy was brought to the attention of the human rights council, the reaction was overwhelmingly supportive. A new human rights policy was already in preparation, and immediately following the conference, the Icelandic host and long-time activist was invited to participate in the drafting of a section addressing weight discrimination. A year later, Reykjavik City became the first Icelandic authority to officially address body size as a social justice issue in one of its charters (Daníelsdóttir 2020).

The Reykjavik Human Rights Policy is broad ranging in its approach. The policy likely provides city employees with greater protection against weight discrimination than can be found in any other workplace in Iceland, as it states that employees may not be dismissed or refused work, career advancement, wage increases or rewards due to their body size or appearance. In addition to banning outright discrimination based on weight, size, or appearance, the policy centers weight in discussions about inclusivity. It asserts the city's responsibilities to create a constructive atmosphere in its workplaces that are free of stereotypes, prejudice and discrimination related to body weight, size, or appearance. It also proclaims workplace health promotion programs should not focus on employees' body build or size but on creating better opportunities for health-promoting behaviors and encouraging social inclusion. Further, the city, in its role as a public authority, employer, and service provider, is required to consider weight diversity when making policy decisions and in the provision of its various services, such that higher-weight people are not unintentionally disadvantaged by structural or systemic inequalities built into everyday life, and that the city and its employees do not inadvertently promote negative attitudes or stereotypes about higher-weight people. It also explicitly states that NGOs concerned with body respect should be consulted when their input might be relevant.

As Iceland's capital city and largest municipality, Reykjavik is home to over a third of the country's population (Statistics Iceland 2019). While not a law, the Reykjavik Human Rights Policy details the city's commitments and responsibilities to social justice as a public authority, employer, and service provider, and influences a wide variety of sectors and services that affect the daily lives of citizens of all ages, including preschool, primary and lower secondary education, social services, housing, child protection, cultural and recreation activities and more. Thus, the reach of the policy is substantial.

Discussion

There are reasons for optimism and pessimism in each of the case studies examined herein. In each, legal and policy efforts to address weight stigma encountered successes and obstacles; there is little doubt that existing structures of weight stigma play a substantial role in the scope of the impediments to addressing weight stigma through laws and policies.

In the UK, the ECJ ruling (and the UK Equality Act 2010) provides scope for other fat individuals to obtain recourse in situations where their work situation is engineered in such a way that they are disadvantaged due to their size. It is likely that many fat people would refrain from taking advantage of such legislation even where it would be applicable to their situation. Rampant cultural fatphobia has resulted in widespread internalization of society's negative attitudes toward fatness, whereby fat individuals blame and shame themselves for their body size (Bombak and Monaghan 2016). As such they may themselves also feel undeserving of protection from discrimination. Further, many fat individuals may be wont to reject the label of "disabled" specifically because of their fatness (Cooper 1997).[10] This reticence to take on the label is a manifestation of ableism, as well as an example of how identity, internalized stigma, and personal beliefs about culpability and mutability function under the constraints of the "deserving disadvantaged" archetype (Kai-Cheong Chan & Gillick, 2009). Indeed, an increase in case law relating to "non-traditional" claimants, properly applied, might serve to broaden understanding of the social model of disability and reduce marginalization and improve treatment across the board. However, as noted above, discrimination on the basis of "disability" can only be invoked when an impairment of some sort is present. Overt discrimination based on animus toward higher-weight individuals is not covered by existing antidiscrimination laws, and, as such, weight needs to receive protected characteristic status in its own right (Wang 2008).

In Michigan, weight has been a protected category under state law since 1976. While this legal shelter has undoubtedly facilitated claims of weight discrimination as well as likely encouraged changed behavior among some employers toward fat people, numerous cases also reflect the well-studied general judicial retrenchment against US antidiscrimination law. That existing stigmas, including weight stigma, contribute to the latter is at least plausible, if difficult to prove. Moreover, difficulty in showing a particular animus is itself a feature of stigma, as the increasing literature on stigma and epistemic injustice document (Buchman, Ho, and Goldberg 2017). Furthermore, the relatively small number of cases brought under ELCRA and in other jurisdictions in the US that provide protection against weight discrimination may, to some extent, reflect the potential social and psychological costs to the plaintiff of exposing themselves to the legal interrogation of their bodies, behaviors, and morals, a discomfiting aspect of exposure that may not be as relevant in discrimination cases against other stigmatized identities (Tirosh 2013).[11]

As noted above, the height and weight protection provided under the ELCRA was originally intended to prevent discrimination on the basis of gender and race and it is likely that many fat residents of Michigan may not even know of the law's existence or its applicability to their situation (Kirkland 2008). As the fat liberation movement gains in strength, and fat rights activists campaign for new laws that protect fat individuals as a class, success of such laws may foster the development of a more politicized fat identity and rising awareness that fat people deserve to be treated on an equal footing to thin people. Importantly, many fat individuals do not identify strongly with fat others and there is a lack of theshared group identity experienced by many other marginalized groups (Crandall 1994). Kirkland (2008) noted that the successful public advocacy campaign to obtain protection against weight-based discrimination in San Francisco in 2000 meant that the fat activists she interviewed from that area had experienced a sense of empowerment and mobilization that would likely be otherwise absent. In interviews with 60 men and women with disabilities, Engel and Munger (2003; as cited in Kirkland 2008) also found that the passing of the Americans with Disabilities Act (ADA) in 1990 produced a sense of empowerment and identity and altered perceptions both from inside and outside the disability community, changing the very way that they interacted with society and their expectations of what life could and should offer. It will be of interest to explore any similar developments among higher-weight individuals in the several jurisdictions where such civil rights battles are currently being fought.

However, many recent attempts to have weight enshrined in law as a distinct protected category have been unsuccessful[12]. Such attempts will need to combat deeply entrenched weight stigma in society, as demonstrated in the UK response to the Kaltoft case. Rulings in jurisdictions where weight is already a protected category further prove that legislators are not immune to these prejudicial ways of thinking about high-weight status. Yet, the relative ease with which weight was included in the 2016 Reykjavik Human Rights Policy demonstrates the importance of Kingdon's (2011) influential concept of "policy windows," which occur when three policy "streams" converge: the problem stream, the politics stream, and the policy stream. As to the *problem* stream, activists, scholars, and City of Reykjavik officials converged on the problem of weight stigma. The centennial marking women's suffrage in Iceland drove a *political* opportunity to focus on problems marginalized groups frequently encounter and the importance of a human rights policy – which was already under preparation in the City – as a locus for developing antidiscrimination protections. Finally, the fact that Reykjavik hosted an important international conference on weight stigma that city officials attended opened up space for discussion on *policy* mechanisms to remedy weight stigma. These three streams converged to create a policy window for explicit protections against weight discrimination in the Reykjavik Human Rights Policy, the proponents of which encountered virtually no resistance in their efforts. In contrast, attempts to enshrine similar protections in the Icelandic constitution have not fared nearly as well, and there again seems little doubt that structural stigma against fat people has at least something to do with the divergence of the policy streams needed to create a policy window on the national, constitutional level.

Ultimately, the analysis herein does not suggest that existing structures of weight stigma in the countries examined render it impossible or even unlikely to use public health law and policy as a tool to counter weight stigma. Quite the contrary; majorities in the US, Canada, Australia, and Iceland support the enactment of specific laws prohibiting weight discrimination (Puhl et al. 2015b). The fact that significant numbers of people in many Western societies seem more ready to adopt such mechanisms does underscore the point that laws and policies tend to *follow* changing social norms than precipitate changes in them. Analysis of attitudes and civil unrest in the United States prior and subsequent to the passing of the Civil Rights Act of 1964 provides further evidence that legislative action requires both a notable proportion of the population in favor of change and a trend of increasing support (Burstein 1979). While support for equal rights continued to increase following the introduction of the Act, it is difficult to conclusively attribute changing public opinion to the legislation per se, rather than to the continuance of the existing trajectory of negative societal attitudes to social injustice. Nevertheless, introduction of the Act provided people of color with protection against overt discrimination and did not hinder further gains in social justice attitudes and beliefs.

While existing legislation prohibiting discrimination based on, for example, race or sex has not eliminated either racism or sexism, such legislation nevertheless proscribes discriminatory behavior and provides recourse where it occurs. Although claims made under this legislation may be difficult to prove, may exact a toll of the plaintiff that could influence the decision to instigate a claim, and are not always successful, some cases nevertheless do succeed, and the development of case law in this area further strengthens the position of marginalized groups.

Perhaps where institutional change may most strongly act as a driver of societal change is in the demonstration of what is considered acceptable behavior – the so-called expressive function of law. Several recent U.S. studies have taken advantage of the changing legislative environment regarding same-sex marriage to explore this phenomenon. In a longitudinal study measuring personal attitudes and perceived social norms toward same-sex marriage at five time points prior to and following the 2015 U.S. Supreme Court ruling that legalized same-sex marriages, participants' perceptions of wider social support for same-sex marriage increased following the ruling, even while individual attitudes were unchanged (Tankard and Paluck 2017). This matters because perceived social norms influence individual behavior, even when they conflict with personal attitudes (Cialdini and Goldstein 2004; Miller and Prentice 2016). Furthermore, perceptions of norms may also motivate changes in attitudes (Stangor, Sechrist, and Jost 2001). Experimental data collected prior to the Supreme Court ruling indicated that both perceived norms and personal attitudes in favor of same-sex marriage were influenced by the likelihood of this legislation passing (Tankard and Paluck 2017).

Support for changes in anti-discrimination legislation that introduces protections for weight status does not nullify concerns that the very stigma made the target of law and policy approaches may create significant friction to the creation, implementation, and enforcement of legal mechanisms. However, work conducted in the US in 2012 and 2013, at a time when a number of states legalized same-sex marriage, suggests that rather than polarizing opinion or prompting a backlash effect, attitude change tended to support both the idea that legislation reflects a changing consensus among a local populace, and that it served to legitimate the issue of same-sex marriage and attitudes toward lesbian, gay, and bisexual individuals, compared with states in which same-sex marriage either remained illegal over this time period, or was already legal and remained so (Flores and Barclay 2016; see also Bishin et al. 2016). The most significant positive changes were among individuals who had previously opposed such legislation, with only a small minority of those previously ambivalent becoming more negative (Flores and Barclay 2016). In terms of changes in legislation conferring protection against discrimination based on weight, the change in the Reykjavik Human Rights policy provides an opportunity to assess changing attitudes. Current efforts to introduce protection based on weight into law in the US state of Massachusetts and the Canadian provinces of Ontario and Manitoba also provide opportunities to empirically assess the impact of such policies.

Some commentators, including the "obesity" organization representatives quoted above, believe that the addition of weight as a protected category would create what is known as a moral hazard, rewarding "bad" behavior and "poor choices." The suggestion is that if we accommodate the needs of fat people, they will not be motivated to try and become thin people. The idea that high-weight status *should* be stigmatized is, unfortunately, not an uncommon belief, even in medical and public health circles, despite evidence that stigmatizing campaigns tend to have the opposite effect to that intended (Vartanian and Smyth 2013). Shaming and discrimination against fat people is endemic throughout Western society, and increasingly everywhere else (Brewis, SturtzSreetharan, and Wutich 2018). In the UK, every single media outlet accompanied their online coverage of the Kaltoft story with what Cooper

(2007) called a "headless fatty" photo – the dehumanized, decapitated, bulging, straining torso, that almost inevitably accompanies any news story involving weight, and demonstrated to increase anti-fat sentiments in readers (Brochu et al. 2013). Fat shaming is light evening entertainment (Ata and Thompson 2010). Yet, the impact of decades of weight stigma, with increasing rates of prejudice and discrimination in the last 10 to 20 years in particular (Brewis, SturtzSreetharan, and Wutich 2018), has been accompanied by increasing rises in BMI worldwide. Further, history has shown that using public health laws in a punitive manner generally serves to broaden existing disparities and injustices, with a concomitant negative impact on health outcomes (Pomeranz 2008). However, the fact that stigma does not "work" is a moot point. In a civil society, the underlying principles of equality and the driving purpose of anti-discrimination legislation is to address systemic forms of bias in society. Legal protections are not intended to provide special treatment for a particular group; rather, they are intended to eliminate existing disadvantage. In this context, a strong case can be made for the addition of weight as a protected category under equality and anti-discrimination laws (Blake and Hatzenbuehler 2019). Systemic anti-fat biases have resulted in barriers to equal opportunity for higher-weight individuals that start in early childhood and are compounded throughout the life course (Daníelsdóttir 2020; Puhl and King 2013). Thus, weight stigma is a fundamental cause of inequality, resulting in economic and health disparities between higher-weight individuals and those whose body weight is considered normative (Goldberg 2017; Hatzenbuehler, Phelan, and Link 2013).

Conclusion

As we have discussed, existing societal weight stigma means that there exists extreme antagonism toward the introduction of protections for higher-weight individuals. Such protections are intended to provide the full access to participation in society that has always been afforded to thin people. The emphasis is not simply on "treating people equally," but on leveraging antidiscrimination and civil rights law to remedy the structural disadvantage fat people so commonly experience in the West (Blake and Hatzenbuehler 2019). For the sake of simplicity, we may return to the reliably contentious chair issue: equity, or true equality, does not dictate that everybody should be made to sit in the same chairs, but that everybody should be able to sit down at work.

When law is used in its expressive function, to change social norms and stipulate new standards of appropriate behavior, the very need for the norm to change means that there will be at least some controversy around such an intervention (McAdams 1997). However, evidence from the US suggests that a critical mass of active and vocal civil rights movements, whose attitudes and goals are, by definition, not aligned with the existing mainstream ethos, can create an impetus for rapid legislative change, which then has a reciprocal relationship on social norms (Burstein 1979; Costain and Majstorovic 1994). The lesson learned from Reykjavik, in particular, is that policy change can happen relatively quickly and uncontroversially when the right information is provided to the right people at the right time. Efforts by the first author to achieve this in the UK via the Government Equalities Office have been hampered predominantly by gatekeeping and lack of awareness of the evidence of widespread systemic inequalities faced by higher-weight people, rather than by anti-fat stigma per se.

Despite widespread anti-fat bias in the Western world, some evidence of cultural shifts against shaming and discrimination, and toward a more just and equal society, suggest that the time may be right to pursue political and social change. While we continue to advocate for policy change at the macro level, we must also continue to challenge fatphobia when it occurs in our daily lives and interactions. Rejecting even apparently minor instances of stigma can serve to signal, and alter, what is considered acceptable behavior (Czopp, Monteith, and Mark 2006; Mallett and Wagner 2011). At the meso level, progress can be made locally, for instance by targeting school anti-bullying policies or local ordinances on employment discrimination – interventions for which there already exists considerable public support (Puhl et al. 2015b). As awareness of the inherent injustice and harmful nature of weight stigma reaches critical mass, the perceived political costs and obstacles may amend themselves toward legal reform.

The role of fat activism in the development of the wide-reaching Reykjavik Human Rights Policy makes it clear that activists and affiliated organizations will continue to be crucial agents in the push against weight stigma. However, such forces, where they even exist, are frequently hampered by lack of funds needed to support concerted policy advocacy and often fail to represent the diversity of individuals affected by anti-fat bias and discrimination (Williams 2017). The burgeoning area of intersectional fat studies scholarship – especially in its overlaps with the areas of critical race/ism, disability, gender, and media studies – signals encouraging movement toward a more widely accessible body liberation space for groups that have long been excluded by hegemonic narratives and perspectives that center fat White people. However, these gains in scholarship must also be accompanied by an equal embrace of the grassroots efforts of fat Black, Indigenous, and other people of color whose humanity and inherent worth must be at the center of our current progress toward fat liberation. As the Black feminist thought-leaders of the Combahee River Collective (1977/2014) made clear decades ago, none of us will be free until all of us are free.

Notes

1. Other legislation addresses discrimination on the basis of sex and race or ethnicity.
2. The word "obesity" is placed in inverted commas to indicate contestation of the medicalization of body weight and the social construction of a disease narrative.
3. Absent from this coverage were the voices of fat rights organizations. It is worth noting that there is no such body in the UK, unlike NAAFA in the US and the Body Respect Association in Iceland (see below), both of whom are often approached for commentary. However, it is at least likely that the BBC did not expect "obesity charities" who claim to cater to the needs of fat people to speak out against the ECJ ruling.
4. Mr. Fry's statement that if employers were to make adjustments to workplace set up to accommodate "very large people," it would "cause friction ... between obese people and other workers" also typifies a common misunderstanding of equality protections as something that gives a disadvantaged group preferential treatment – that they are getting something more than their benighted "normal" colleagues, rather than access to equal opportunities.
5. See for example, the opinions of the Advocate Generals in ECJ rulings on *HK Danmark* (Cases C-335/11 and C-337/11; point 32) and *Kaltoft* (Case C-354/13; point 32) and HM Government Office for Disability Issues (2011) Guidance on the Equality Act (2010), paragraph A3.
6. As such, the situation remains the same after the UK left the European Union in 2020. The Equality Act (2010) covers this same ground, even in the absence of EU statutory requirements.
7. Wilkes criticizes the formation of what she terms HIPAA culture, but herein we take no position on the merits of the critique. Our point is rather the ways in which changes in law can have downstream effects independent of the specific ways the laws are and are not enforced. On HIPAA privacy in general, see the body of work from legal scholar Stacey Tovino (2017).
8. Confidence in the extent to which structural stigma is influencing judicial decision-making can only follow (1) the development of a valid and reliable construct for identifying when such stigma exists and/or is animating particular judicial reasoning; and (2) an ensuing legal surveillance or mapping study that will document the prevalence of such stigma in the common law. Neither step has been achieved, though Goldberg is working on a construct for tracing stigma in statutory and regulatory language.
9. https://stigmaconference.com/previous-conferences/reykjavik-2015/
10. It should be noted that many higher-weight individuals may also reject a fat identity, considering themselves as atypical of "other" fat people and being, in truth, a thin person in a temporarily fat body (Kyrölä and Harjunen 2017).
11. orality and value judgments frequently play a role in the negative experiences of women and Black and Indigenous people of color in the legal system. For a thorough examination of how multiple systems of oppression impact minoritized groups, see Gonzalez Van Cleve (2016) and Matsuda (1991).
12. For example, in the US states of Utah, Massachusetts, and New York, the city of Las Vegas, and in the Canadian provinces of Manitoba and Ontario.

Acknowledgments

The authors would like to thank Darliene Howell (NAAFA Board of Directors), Andrea LaMarre, Michael Orsini, Cat Pausé, Jaclyn Siegel, Joslyn Smith, Iyiola Solanke, and the members of the Fat Studies Facebook group for comments and suggestions.

Disclosure statement

No potential conflict of interest was reported by the authors.

ORCID

Angela Meadows http://orcid.org/0000-0002-6273-7564

Funding

Angela Meadows is supported by a SSHRC Banting Postdoctoral Fellowship [award no. 411947-64696]. Marquisele Mercedes is supported by a Presidential Fellowship from Brown University.

References

Adamitis, E. M. 2000. "Appearance Matters: A Proposal to Prohibit Appearance Discrimination in Employment." *Washington Law Review* 75 (1):198–223.

Ailshire, J. A., and J. S. House. 2011. "The Unequal Burden of Weight Gain: An Intersectional Approach to Understanding Social Disparities in BMI Trajectories from 1986 to 2001/2002." *Social Forces* 90 (2):397–423. doi:10.1093/sf/sor001.

Asgeirsdottir, B. B., G. Ingolfsdottir, and I. D. Sigfusdottir. 2012. "Body Image Trends among Icelandic Adolescents: A Cross-sectional National Study from 1997 to 2010." *Body Image* 9 (3):404–08. doi:10.1016/j.bodyim.2012.02.002.

Ata, R. N., and J. K. Thompson. 2010. "Weight Bias in the Media: A Review of Recent Research." *Obesity Facts* 3 (1):41–46. doi:10.1159/000276547.

Barnes, C. 2012. "Understanding the Social Model of Disability." In *The Routledge Handbook of Disability Studies*, edited by N. Watson, A. Roulstone, and C. Thomas, 1st ed., 12–29. London: Routledge.

BBC News. 2014, December 18. "Obesity 'Could Be a Disability' – EU Courts Rule." https://www.bbc.co.uk/news/health-30529791 .

Bishin, B. G., T. J. Hayes, M. B. Incantalupo, and C. A. Smith. 2016. "Opinion Backlash and Public Attitudes: Are Political Advances in Gay Rights Counterproductive?" *American Journal of Political Science* 60 (3):625–48. doi:10.1111/ajps.12181.

Blake, V. K., and M. L. Hatzenbuehler. 2019. "Legal Remedies to Address Stigma-based Health Inequalities in the United States: Challenges and Opportunities." *The Milbank Quarterly* 97 (2):480–504. doi:10.1111/1468-0009.12391.

Bombak, A. E., and L. F. Monaghan. 2016. "Obesity, Bodily Change and Health Identities: A Qualitative Study of Canadian Women." *Sociology of Health & Illness* 39 (6):923–40. doi:10.1111/1467-9566.12537.

Brewis, A., C. SturtzSreetharan, and A. Wutich. 2018. "Obesity Stigma as a Globalizing Health Challenge." *Global Health* 14:20. doi:10.1186/s12992-018-0337-x.

Brochu, P. M., R. L. Pearl, R. M. Puhl, and K. D. Brownell. 2013. "Do Media Portrayals of Obesity Influence Support for Weight-related Medical Policy?" *Health Psychology* 33 (2):197–200. doi:10.1037/a0032592.

Buchman, D. Z., A. Ho, and D. S. Goldberg. 2017. "Investigating Trust, Expertise, and Epistemic Injustice in Chronic Pain." *Bioethical Inquiry* 14 (1):31–42. doi:10.1007/s11673-016-9761-x.

Burris, S. 2002. "Disease Stigma in U.S. Public Health Law." *Journal of Law, Medicine & Ethics* 30 (2):179–90. doi:10.1111/j.1748-720X.2002.tb00385.x.

Burstein, P. 1979. "Public Opinion, Demonstrations, and the Passage of Antidiscrimination Legislation." *Public Opinion Quarterly* 43 (2):157–72. doi:10.1086/268508.

Calogero, R. M., T. L. Tylka, J. L. Mensinger, A. Meadows, and S. Daníelsdóttir. 2019. "Recognizing the Fundamental Right to Be Fat: A Weight-inclusive Approach to Size Acceptance and Healing from Sizeism." *Women & Therapy* 42 (1–2):22–44. doi:10.1080/02703149.2018.1524067.

Campos, P., A. Saguy, P. Ernsberger, E. Oliver, and G. Gaesser. 2006. "The Epidemiology of Overweight and Obesity? Public Health Crisis or Moral Panic?" *International Journal of Epidemiology* 35 (1):55–60. doi:10.1093/ije/dyi254.

Cialdini, R. B., and N. J. Goldstein. 2004. "Social Influence: Compliance and Conformity." *Annual Review of Psychology* 55 (1):591–621. doi:10.1146/annurev.psych.55.090902.142015.

Ciciurkaite, C., and B. L. Perry. 2018. "Body Weight, Perceived Weight Stigma and Mental Health among Women at the Intersection of Race/ethnicity and Socioeconomic Status: Insights from the Modified Labelling Approach." *Sociology of Health & Illness* 40 (1):18–37. doi:10.1111/1467-9566.12619.

City of Reykjavik. 2016. "Human Rights Policy." https://reykjavik.is/en/city-of-reykjaviks-human-rights-policy .

Clarke, J. A. 2015. "Against Immutability." *Yale Law Journal* 125 (1):2–102.

Combahee River Collective. 2014. "A Black Feminist Statement." *Women's Studies Quarterly* 42 (3–4):271–80. (Original work published 1977) doi:10.1353/wsq.2014.0052.

Cooper, C. 1997. "Can a Fat Woman Call Herself Disabled?" *Disability & Society* 12 (1):31–42. doi:10.1080/09687599727443.

Cooper, C. 2007. "January." *Headless Fatties.* http://charlottecooper.net/fat/fat-writing/headless-fatties-01-07/ .

Costain, A. N., and S. Majstorovic. 1994. "Congress, Social Movements and Public Opinion: Multiple Origins of Women's Rights Legislation." *Political Research Quarterly* 47 (1):111–35. doi:10.1177/106591299404700106.

Cox, J. A. 2020. *Fat Girls in Black Bodies.* Berkeley: North Atlantic Books.

Crandall, C. S. 1994. "Prejudice against Fat People: Ideology and Self-interest." *Journal of Personality and Social Psychology* 66 (5):882–94. doi:10.1037/0022-3514.66.5.882.

Crenshaw, K. 1991. "Mapping the Margins: Intersectionality, Identity Politics, and Violence against Women of Color." *Stanford Law Review* 43 (6):1241–99. doi:10.2307/1229039.

Czopp, A. M., M. J. Monteith, and A. Y. Mark. 2006. "Standing up for a Change: Reducing Bias through Interpersonal Confrontation." *Journal of Personality and Social Psychology* 90 (5):784–803. doi:10.1037/0022-3514.90.5.784.

Daníelsdóttir, S. 2020. "Understanding Body Respect as a Social Justice Issue for Young People." In *Social Justice for Children and Young People: International Perspectives*, edited by C. S. Clauss-Ehlers, A. B. Sood, and M. D. Weist, 228–43. Cambridge: Cambridge University Press.

Danielsdottir, S., and S.H. Jonsson. 2015. *Fordómar Á Grundvelli Holdafars Í Íslensku Samfélagi*. Reykjavik: Directorate of Health. https://www.landlaeknir.is/utgefid-efni/skjal/item28261/ .

Daufin, E. K. 2020. "Thick Sistahs and Heavy Disprivilege: Black Women, Intersectionality, and Weight Stigma." In *Thickening Fat: Fat Bodies, Intersectionality, and Social Justice*, edited by M. Friedman, C. Rice, and J. Rinaldi, 160–70. New York: Routledge.

Dred Scott v. Sandford. 60 U.S. (19 How.) 393. 1857.

Elliott-Larsen Civil Rights Act. 1976. "§37.2202 Employer; Prohibited Practices; Exemptions." http://legislature.mi.gov/doc.aspx?mcl-37-2202 .

Engel, David M., & Frank W. Munger (2003). Rights of Inclusion: Law and Identity in the Life Stories of Americans with Disabilities. Chicago: Univ. of Chicago Press

Equal Employment Commission. 2012, April 10. "Resources for Human Development Settles EEOC Disability Suit for $125,000 [Press Release]." https://www.eeoc.gov/newsroom/resources-human-development-settles-eeoc-disability-suit-125000 .

Equality Act 2010, c.15. http://www.legislation.gov.uk/ukpga/2010/15/contents .

Evans, J., B. Davies, and E. Rich. 2008. "The Class and Cultural Functions of Obesity Discourse: Our Latter Day Child Saving Movement." *International Studies in Sociology of Education* 18 (2):117–32. doi:10.1080/09620210802351367.

Farino v. Renaissance Club, Lexis 1184. Mich. Ct. App. 1999.

Flores, A. R., and S. Barclay. 2016. "Backlash, Consensus, Legitimacy or Polarization: The Effect of Same-sex Marriage Policy on Mass Attitudes." *Political Research Quarterly* 69 (1):43–56. doi:10.1177/1065912915621175.

Goldberg, D. S. 2017. "On Stigma & Health." *The Journal of Law, Medicine & Ethics* 45 (4):475–83. doi:10.1177/1073110517750581.

Gonzalez Van Cleve, N. 2016. *Crook County: Racism and Injustice in America's Largest Criminal Court*. Stanford: Stanford University Press.

Harris v. Hutcheson, Lexis 131. Mich. Ct. App. 2018.

Hatzenbuehler, M. L., J. C. Phelan, and B. G. Link. 2013. "Stigma as a Fundamental Cause of Population Health Inequalities." *American Journal of Public Health* 103 (5):813–21. doi:10.2105/AJPH.2012.301069.

Hatzenbuehler, M. L., K. M. Keyes, and D. S. Hasin. 2009. "Associations between Perceived Weight Discrimination and the Prevalence of Psychiatric Disorders in the General Population." *Obesity* 17 (11):2033–39. doi:10.1038/oby.2009.131.

Herndon, A. 2002. "Disparate but Disabled: Fat Embodiment and Disability Studies." *NWSA Journal* 14 (3):120–37. doi:10.1353/nwsa.2003.0007.

Hicken, M. T., H. Lee, and A. K. Hing. 2018. "The Weight of Racism: Vigilance and Racial Inequalities in Weight-related Measures." *Social Science & Medicine* 199:157–66. doi:10.1016/j.socscimed.2017.03.058.

Hill Collins, P., and S. Bilge. 2016. *Intersectionality*. Cambridge: Polity Press.

HK Danmark. 2012. EU:C:EU:C:2012:775, AG Kokott opinion. https://eur-lex.europa.eu/legal-content/EN/TXT/?qid=1600655318376&uri=CELEX:62011CC0335 .

HM Government Office for Disability Issues. 2011. *Disability: Equality Act 2010 – Guidance on Matters to Be Taken into Account in Determining Questions Relating to the Definition of Disability*. https://assets.publishing.service.gov.uk/government/uploads/system/uploads/attachment_data/file/570382/Equality_Act_2010-disability_definition.pdf .

Ingolfsdottir, G., B. B. Asgeirsdottir, T. Gunnarsdottir, and A. S. Bjornsson. 2014. "Changes in Body Image and Dieting among 16–19-year-old Icelandic Students from 2000 to 2010." *Body Image* 11 (4):364–69. doi:10.1016/j.bodyim.2014.05.006.

Kai-Cheong Chan, N., and A. C. Gillick. 2009. "Fatness as a Disability: Questions of Personal and Group Identity." *Disability & Society* 24 (2):231–43. doi:10.1080/09687590802652520.

Kaltoft v Municipality of Billund. 2014. C-354/13, EU:C:2014:2463. https://eur-lex.europa.eu/legal-content/EN/TXT/?qid=1600655454371&uri=CELEX:62013CJ0354 .

Kaplan, D. 2000. "The Definition of Disability: Perspective of the Disability Community." *Journal of Health Care Law & Policy* 3 (2):352–64. Available at: http://digitalcommons.law.umaryland.edu/jhclp/vol3/iss2/5 .

Kasten, G. 2018. "Listen … and Speak: A Discussion of Weight Bias, Its Intersections with Homophobia, Racism, and Misogyny, and Their Impacts on Health." *Canadian Journal of Dietetic Practice and Research* 79 (3):133–38. doi:10.3148/cjdpr–2018–023.

Keith, V. M., A. W. Nguyen, R. J. Taylor, L. M. Chatters, and D. M. Mouzon. 2017. "Microaggressions, Discrimination, and Phenotype among African Americans: A Latent Class Analysis of the Impact of Skin Tone and BMI." *Sociological Inquiry* 87 (2):233–55. doi:10.1111/soin.12168.

Kingdon, J. W. 2011. *Agendas, Alternatives, and Public Policies*. 2nd ed. Boston: Longman.

Kirkland, A. 2008. "Think of the Hippopotamus: Rights Consciousness in the Fat Acceptance Movement." *Law & Society Review* 42 (2):397–432. doi:10.1111/j.1540-5893.2008.00346.x.

Korematsu v. United States, 323 U.S. 214. 1944.

Kristen, E. 2002. "Addressing the Problem of Weight Discrimination in Employment." *California Law Review* 90 (1):57–109. doi:10.15779/Z38BT62.

Kyrölä, K., and H. Harjunen. 2017. "Phantom/liminal Fat and Feminist Theories of the Body." *Feminist Theory* 18 (2):99–117. doi:10.1177/1464700117700035.

Lamoria v. Health Care & Retirement Corp., 584 N.W. 2d 589. Mich. Ct. App. 1998.

Link, B. G., and J. Phelan. 2014. "Stigma Power." *Social Science & Medicine* 103:24–32. doi:10.1016/j.socscimed.2013.07.035.

Link, B. G., and J. C. Phelan. 2001. "Conceptualizing Stigma." *Annual Review of Sociology* 27 (1):363–85. doi:10.1146/annurev.soc.27.1.363.

Makowski, A. C., T. J. Kim, C. Luck-Sikorski, and O von Dem Knesebeck. 2019. "Social Deprivation, Gender and Obesity: Multiple Stigma? Results of a Population Survey from Germany." *BMJ Open* 9:e023389. doi:10.1136/bmjopen–2018–023389.

Mallett, R. K., and D. E. Wagner. 2011. "The Unexpectedly Positive Consequences of Confronting Sexism." *Journal of Experimental Social Psychology* 47 (1):215–20. doi:10.1016/j.jesp.2010.10.001.

Matsuda, M. J. 1991. "Voices of America: Accent, Antidiscrimination Law, and a Jurisprudence for the Last Reconstruction." *Yale Law Journal* 100 (5):1329–407. doi:10.2307/796694.

McAdams, R. H. 1997. "The Origin, Development, and Regulation of Norms." *Michigan Law Review* 96 (2):338–433. doi:10.2307/1290070.

Miller, D. T., and D. A. Prentice. 2016. "Changing Norms to Change Behavior." *Annual Review of Psychology* 67 (1):339–61. doi:10.1146/annurev-psych–010814–015013.

Mollow, A. 2015. "Disability Studies Gets Fat." *Hypatia* 30 (1):199–216. doi:10.1111/hypa.12126.

Pomeranz, J. L. 2008. "A Historical Analysis of Public Health, the Law, and Stigmatized Social Groups: The Need for Both Obesity and Weight Bias Legislation." *Obesity* 16 (Suppl 2):S93–S103. doi:10.1038/oby.2008.452.

Puhl, R. M., J. D. Latner, K. O'Brien, J. Luedicke, S. Danielsdottir, and M. Forhan. 2015a. "A Multinational Examination of Weight Bias: Predictors of Anti-fat Attitudes across Four Countries." *International Journal of Obesity* 39 (7):1166–73. doi:10.1038/ijo.2015.32.

Puhl, R. M., J. D. Latner, K. S. O'Brien, J. Luedicke, S. Danielsdottir, and X. Ramos Salas. 2015b. "Potential Policies and Laws to Prohibit Weight Discrimination: Public Views from 4 Countries." *The Millbank Quarterly* 93 (4):691–731. doi:10.1111/1468-0009.12162.

Puhl, R. M., and K. M. King. 2013. "Weight Discrimination and Bullying." *Best Practice & Research Clinical Endocrinology & Metabolism* 27 (2):117–27. doi:10.1016/j.beem.2012.12.002.

Reece, R. L. 2018. "Coloring Weight Stigma: On Race, Colorism, Weight Stigma, and the Failure of Additive Intersectionality." *Sociology of Race and Ethnicity* 5 (3):388–400. doi:10.1177/2332649218795185.

Rice, C., K. Pendleton Jiménez, E. Harrison, M. Robinson, J. Rinaldi, A. LaMarre, and J. Andrew. 2020. "Bodies at the Intersections: Refiguring Intersectionality through Queer Women's Complex Embodiments." *Signs: Journal of Women in Culture and Society* 46 (1):177–200. doi:10.1086/709219.

Ross v. Beaumont Hosp., 687 F. Supp. 1115. E.D. Mich. 1988.

Rothblum, E. D. 2018. "Slim Chance for Permanent Weight Loss." *Archives of Scientific Psychology* 6 (1):63–69. doi:10.1037/arc0000043.

Schweik, S. M. 2009. *The Ugly Laws: Disability in Public*. vol. 3. New York: NYU Press.

Silverman, R. D., and W. F. Wiley. 2017. "Shaming Vaccine Refusal." *Journal of Law, Medicine & Ethics* 45 (4):569–81. doi:10.1177/1073110517750597.

Soifer, A. 2003. "Disabling the ADA: Essences, Better Angels, and Unprincipled Neutrality Claims." *William & Mary Law Review* 44 (3):1285–340. doi:10.2139/ssrn.389400.

Stangor, C., G. B. Sechrist, and J. T. Jost. 2001. "Changing Racial Beliefs by Providing Consensus Information." *Personality and Social Psychology Bulletin* 27 (4):486–96. doi:10.1177/0146167201274009.

Statistics Iceland. 2019. *Statistical Series: Population Development 2018*. Reykjavik: Statistics Iceland.

Strings, S. 2015. "Obese Black Women as "Social Dead Weight": Reinventing the "Diseased Black Woman"." *Signs: Journal of Women in Culture and Society* 41 (1):107–30. doi:10.1086/681773.

Strings, S. 2019. *Fearing the Black Body: The Racial Origins of Fat Phobia*. New York: NYU Press.

Tankard, M. E., and E. L. Paluck. 2017. "The Effect of a Supreme Court Decision regarding Gay Marriage on Social Norms and Personal Attitudes." *Psychological Science* 28 (9):1334–44. doi:10.1177/0956797617709594.

Tirosh, Y. 2013. "The Right to Be Fat." *Yale Journal of Health Policy, Law, and Ethics* 12 (2):264–335. http://digitalcommons.law.yale.edu/yjhple/vol12/iss2/2 .

Tovino, S. A. 2017. "The HIPAA Privacy Rule and the EU GDPR: Illustrative Comparisons." *Seton Hall Law Review* 47 (4):973–93. http://scholars.law.unlv.edu/facpub/1066 .

van Amsterdam, N. 2013. "Big Fat Inequalities, Thin Privilege: An Intersectional Perspective on 'Body Size'." *European Journal of Women's Studies* 20 (2):155–69. doi:10.1177/1350506812456461.

Vartanian, L. R., and J. M. Smyth. 2013. "Primum Non Nocere: Obesity Stigma and Public Health." *Journal of Bioethical Inquiry* 10 (1):49–57. doi:10.1007/s11673-012-9412-9.

Wang, L. 2008. "Weight Discrimination: One Size Fits All Remedy?" *Yale Law Journal* 117 (8):1900–45. doi:10.2307/20454697.

Webb v. Swartz Creek Community Schils., Lexis 742. Mich. Ct. App. 2001.

Wilkes, J. J. 2014. "The Creation of HIPAA Culture: Prioritizing Privacy Paranoia over Patient Care." *Brigham Young University Law Review* 2014 (5):1213–49. Available at: https://digitalcommons.law.byu.edu/lawreview/vol2014/iss5/7 .

Williams, A. A. 2017. "*Fat People of Color*: Emergent Intersectional Discourse Online." *Social Sciences* 6 (1):15. doi:10.3390/socsci6010015.

OPEN ACCESS

The anti-stigma principle and legal protection from fattism

Iyiola Solanke

ABSTRACT

'Fattism" has been described as the last acceptable prejudice. Discrimination on the grounds of weight is experienced regularly by women and men in relation to employment as well as access to goods and services. As I show in this article, it can also be seen as a form of intersectional discrimination. Yet a legal remedy for weight discrimination exists in just a few countries. In this essay, I consider why legal protection is so limited: I highlight the influence of the logic of immutability and suggest that an alternative logic – an anti-stigma principle – should be used to guide the evolution of anti-weight discrimination law.

Introduction

Once again, during COVID-19, "obesity" has been defined as a significant problem and a major threat to public health (Editorial in The Lancet 2020; Crawford and Jeffery 2005). Little attention is paid to "fattism," discrimination experienced by people who are regularly described as "fat," "overweight," "obese" or living with "obesity." Weight discrimination occurs in employment and access to services, especially healthcare, but this is rarely prohibited by law. Any legal remedy secured by a target of weight discrimination is usually derived through the use of disability discrimination law.

This article argues for specific legal protection against weight discrimination, or "fattism." Like Tirosh (2012), I propose a move toward a new legal paradigm. The argument is set out in four parts. First, I explore the impact of the idea of immutability on the evolution of anti-discrimination law. I then outline the limitations created by the idea of immutability in relation to the personal scope of anti-discrimination law, including intersectional discrimination. Following this, I propose that immutability be replaced by an anti-stigma principle and illustrate briefly how this application would look in relation to weight discrimination. As will be seen, the anti-stigma principle not only offers a legal remedy for weight discrimination but also for intersectional discrimination, meaning that equality law could provide protection for an especially vulnerable group of workers – fat Black women (Lien et al. 2008).

Fattism

The world is fatphobic, despite the increasing number of fat people (Editorial 2020). Being fat is regarded as something to be feared and avoided, especially for women. In particular, the young are fatphobic – Solbes and Enesco (2010) concluded that

> "children who grow up in Western societies idealize thinness from an early age and denigrate overweight, to which they associate explicitly and implicitly a series of negative traits that have nothing to do with the weight. As they grow older, they seem to reduce their levels of explicit prejudice, but not the intensity of implicit bias."

A fatphobic child has a higher likelihood to mature into a fatphobic adult.

It is therefore worrying that little attention is paid to the everyday discrimination experienced by those who are fat (Farr 2018). Public accommodations – seating in restaurants, cafés and waiting rooms or toilets in concert halls, airplanes and bus stations – are rarely designed to accommodate "overweight" or "obese" bodies. Some U.S. airlines require fat passengers to purchase a second seat at the same price as the first (Bolton 2004; Higginbotham 2003).

Many studies have identified and illustrated the detrimental impact of body size on income and earning (Atella et al. 2007; Baum, Charles, and Ford 2004; Cawley 2004; MacClean and Moon 1980), albeit mostly focusing on White women (Judge and Cable 2011). Lempert (2007) concludes that the wage "bias against weight has increased, despite drastic increases in the rate of 'obesity' in the United States" yet simultaneously "the increasing rarity of thinness has led to its rising premium." Rausch (2013) has written about the fat premium in insurance. Gortmaker et al. (1993) suggested that discrimination may account for the reduced social and economic status of "overweight" adolescents and young adults. Mason (2012) later illustrated that discrimination does indeed play a role in income inequality in the USA. Further studies have found that weight discrimination is getting worse (Andreyeva, Puhl, and Brownell 2008; Roehling 2002).

Fat is a black feminist issue

The prevalence of fatness in the population varies by race and ethnicity – weight discrimination is an intersectional issue.[1] Among African Americans, 28.6% are classified as "obese," compared with 21% of Hispanics and 18% of Whites (Bell, McLaughlin, and Sequeira 2004). Black women in particular are more likely to be "overweight" than men – in the USA, about 40% of Black, Hispanic and Native American women are described as "obese" (Bell and McLaughlin 2006). Despite this, women of color are rarely the focus of or included in studies on body weight and size due to assumptions that these women have a more positive approach to their body size. A study by the University of Arizona claimed that 70% of Black girls were satisfied with their bodies compared to 90% of White girls who were dissatisfied with their size (Critser 2003). Media depictions also stereotype fat Black women – fatness is perceived to be a consequences of bad choices. This depiction also sends a message about race as well as class – fatness is viewed as a consequence of immorality for the poor but the result of illness among the wealthy (Saguy and Gruys 2010).

Shaw describes the "triple fetishization" of the fat, Black, female body that signifies "the primal, the erotic and the exotic" (Shaw 2006, 49). An internalization of this historical fetishization may explain why Black women are more comfortable with their weight than White women. It may also be that among persistently impoverished Black communities, fat symbolizes wealth while thinness still equates to poverty. Furthermore, Black women may have a broader definition of attractiveness and find greater size acceptance within their communities than White women do within White communities.

However, this higher acceptance of fatness ultimately leaves Black women more vulnerable to weight discrimination in the labor market: first, the portrayal of the successful career woman is White and thin (Tempesta and Siebert 2016) and second, employer standards on size will negatively affect more women of color. This argument was raised by an African American woman denied a trainee waitress job because her hip measurements exceeded the maximum allowed by the employer's purportedly neutral height and weight chart. She complained of indirect discrimination, arguing that due to genetic differences, the employer's hip measurement standard had a disproportionate impact on African American women (Roehling 2002). Additionally, employer weight bias is more likely to apply to more Black women as they are less likely to be in hiring and firing positions (Bell and McLaughlin 2006): there are, statistically speaking, more White male and female managers who are fatphobic and more Black women workers who are fat. Fat Black women are more excluded than fat White women: fatness has more consequences for Black women in the labor market.

Despite the prevalence of weight discrimination in society, there are few jurisdictions that provide legal protection. There has never been legal protection against weight discrimination in the UK and in Europe. In the USA, only one state – Michigan – explicitly bans weight discrimination. Across Europe the prohibition against "body build and type" introduced by the city of Reykjavik (Iceland) stands alone.[2] There is increasing support for the need to make weight a protected ground in anti-discrimination law (Rubino et al. 2020). According to Suh et al. (2014, 1872), "there is strong, consistent support for policies prohibiting weight discrimination." Puhl et al. suggest public support for specific anti-weight discrimination law (2014). The Lancet (Editorial 2020) also argues that the time has come for serious action. Even the American Society for Metabolic and Bariatric Surgery (ASMBS) has called for the US government to take action to reduce weight stigma and discrimination (Wolfe 2012). Yet governments have done little to protect individuals from discrimination based on body shape and size. In contrast, regulatory suggestions have included proposals that fat people be put in prison camps or that discrimination against fat people be legalized in insurance, work and education (Byrd 2004). As I illustrate below, fatphobia is inherent in the logic of anti-discrimination law.

The logic of anti-discrimination law: immutability

Why are there so few places with a legal prohibition against weight discrimination? Reliance on the logic of immutability might explain this. Immutability describes something that is not chosen and cannot be changed: to be immutable is not merely to be unchanging, but also to be *unable* to change. It suggests irrefutability, perpetuity and irreversibility. Perhaps most importantly for anti-discrimination law, it strongly suggests the absence of blame – people have not chosen their skin color or sex so should not be blamed for this. Victims of discrimination have no control and are therefore "innocent," deserving of state protection through the use of law.

This idea plays a central role in determining where the anti-discrimination principle should be active. According to Marcosson (2001),

> "few arguments offered on behalf of ending discrimination or inequality resonate more powerfully than immutability. It reflects the universal appeal of the concept that it is unfair to disadvantage people based on a characteristic over which they exercise no control."

Legal protection is limited to those suffering mistreatment for attributes that are immutable – immutability guides the personal scope of anti-discrimination law in the UK, EU and USA: protection focuses on characteristics similar to sex that are "innate and largely immutable … closely connected with an individual's personality and life chances."[3] In *TEST-Achat*[4]. AG Kokott described race, ethnic origin and gender as characteristics that are "inseparably linked'" to an individual "over which he has no influence" and that are "not subject to any natural changes." In *Frontiero*, the US Supreme Court clarified that immutability suggests a group defined by a permanent and unchanging feature "determined solely by accident of birth."[5] Accordingly, race, gender and national origin are treated as immutable characteristics (Darmer and Katherine 2010). Yet the consequences (Shapiro 2002) of this very literal approach were seen in *Rogers*, where the Supreme Court argued that a braided hairstyle was mutable as it could easily be changed but an Afro was natural and thus immutable (Turner 2001).

Immutability has helped to extend legal protection to sexual orientation discrimination in the USA (Clarke 2015). State courts in Wisconsin,[6] Texas,[7] Michigan[8].and California[9]. and supreme courts in New Mexico,[10] Iowa,[11] California[12]. and Connecticut[13]. all accepted a new approach to immutability linked not to permanent and unchanging but *fundamental* characteristics. For example, in *Latta*[14]. a District Court stated "s]exual orientation and sexual identity are immutable; they are so fundamental to one's identity that a person should not be required to abandon them." In *Obergefell I*[15]. the US Supreme Court confirmed that immutability arises not only where a characteristic is "strictly unchangeable" but also where "the characteristic is a core trait or condition that one cannot or should not be required to abandon." In *Obergefell II*,[16] the Supreme Court accepted the submission from the American Psychological Association that sexual orientation should be seen as a core trait that one "cannot or should not be required to abandon" and that "[m]ost gay men and lesbians do not experience their sexual orientation as a voluntary choice."

However, some argue immutability should be discarded (Gill 2014; Goldberg 2004; Hutchinson 2003; Mucciaroni and Killian 2004; Stein 2011). Darmer and Katherine (2010) states:

> "[it] is not only inherently stigmatizing to ask whether a person's sexual orientation can be 'changed' but this approach to sexual orientation also suggests a heterosexual norm: heterosexuality is the 'preferred' sexual orientation and that it would be better if folks could change their sexual orientation if it deviates from that norm."

Immutability suggests a norm with the subtext that those who cannot satisfy it will be "tolerated" and even "forgiven" as their deviation (skin color, sex, sexual orientation or impairment) is not their "fault" – they did not choose the "deviation" and can do nothing to change it. Immutability suggests a kind of paternalistic social forgiveness for the "misfortune" of being fat, Black, female, disabled or gay, rather than an acceptance of the legitimacy of these attributes. Immutability therefore does nothing to tackle the stigma attached to various attributes, but, in fact, supports that stigma. It makes the characteristic the problem, rather than the social meaning given to it.

Furthermore, immutability enables society to continue to "punish" those considered to *choose* not to subscribe to its norms, such as fat people. Weight discrimination is apparently acceptable due to the widespread belief that fat is mutable and thus fat people have only themselves to blame.

Intersectional discrimination

The link between immutability and anti-discrimination law may explain the absence of legal protection against weight discrimination. Immutability has also encouraged discrimination to be approached as zero-sum, with complaints made on one or the other ground – e.g. race or sex – but not both combined. Equality campaigns were also designed in this way: the Suffragists excluded voting rights for Black and poor women – Black women were conspicuously absent at the U.S. Seneca Falls Anti-Slavery Convention of 1848 where mainly middle-class White delegates debated women's suffrage. As Anna Julia Cooper (1892, 1988) wrote, "the White woman could at least plead for her own emancipation; the Black woman, doubly enslaved, could but suffer and struggle and be silent." Sojourner Truth asked "ain't I a woman" to challenge the exclusion of Black women from the suffragists.

This zero-sum approach was challenged in the 20th century by critical race feminist arguments that Black women have no choice as to which attribute is the source of discrimination and thus should not be forced to choose in order to secure a legal remedy. Critical race feminists developed and applied critical race theory to consider "the interactive relationship between racism and sexism from the experiential standpoint and knowledge base of Black women" – and develop legal theories grounded in that specific reality. One such theory is "intersectionality," a term coined by Crenshaw (1989) to crystallize the particular position of Black women workers in the labor market.

In *Degraffenreid*[17]. a group of Black women at General Motors (GM), the largest employer in St Louis, complained of discrimination due to the synergy of race and gender. In 1977, 22% of the population in Louisiana were Black women, yet prior to 1970, GM employed just one Black woman as a janitor. In total, GM hired just 6 Black female workers in 1970, 11 in 1971, none in 1972, and 137 in 1973. By late 1973, GM had 155 Black women workers out of a total workforce of 8,500. Yet by January 1974, all of GM's Black women workers had been made redundant: as the most recent recruits ("last in"), they were the first to be fired ("first out"). Only the Black female janitor remained.

However, during this time, GM hired Black men and White women and thus a claim of race or sex discrimination alone would have been unsuccessful. The only way to secure a remedy was to ask the court to recognize that the situation of Black women was qualitatively different from both of these groups because of a synergy between race and gender. Although the law took race and sex separately, they argued that in their existence as Black women, racism and sexism converged, resulting in a "synergistic" combination of two degraded statuses: "[...] the disabilities of Blacks and the disabilities which inhere in their status as women resulting in a condition "more terrible than the sum of their two constituent parts" (Scales-Trent 1989, 1). The concept of intersectional discrimination was devised to crystallize this. Degraffenreid argued that the experience of employment discrimination arose in the wake (Sharpe 2016) of slavery from the combination of societal racism, GM's racist employment practices, and the trade-union sanctioned seniority system. She asked the court to recognize the synergy in her status as a Black woman per se, as an "integrated, undifferentiated, complete whole" (Austin 1989, 540), who lived in society as "twice-stigmatised . . . twice kin to the despised majority of all the human life that there is" (Jordan 1981, 140).

This synergy is at the core of intersectionality, emphasizing the effects produced when two or more elements work together. In the absence of synergy, the idea of intersectional discrimination loses its social and political context. It is reduced to identity politics – the prospect of potentially unlimited "combination" of characteristics emerges and the systemic critique is lost. Without synergy, intersectionality is just another name for multiple discrimination. Under "multiple discrimination," discrimination is additive (experienced in a single event) or cumulative (occurring at separate events) (Hannett 2003). These forms of multiple discrimination can generally be described as sex- or race- "plus" (Scales-Trent 1989). As these two forms are aggregative rather than synergistic, they differ significantly from intersectionality.

A similar argument was raised in *Jefferies v Harris County Commission*,[18] where a Black woman employee claimed discrimination when she was refused promotion to a job that had previously been held by a White woman and a Black man. *Jeffries* was not denied employment or threatened with dismissal – her job was secure – and there was no evidence of sex discrimination or race discrimination. However, she argued that she was subject to a "cement ceiling" created by discriminatory stereotypes based on her race and gender.

The US District Court rejected *Degraffenreid* as seeking a "super-remedy." However, in *Jeffries*, the US Federal Appeal Court ordered a reconsideration of the intersectional race and sex discrimination aspects of the complaint: it refused to accept a result that left Black women workers – a significant proportion of the active labor force – vulnerable and without a remedy for discrimination.[19]

The concept of intersectionality was neither an abstract matter nor simple identity politics. The demand for legal recognition of the labor market position of Black women workers arose from a structural critique of political, economic and social organization with origins in the philosophy developed from the experiences of African women enslaved in America, who were beaten, lynched and raped to give birth to children who would be used as products to perpetuate the slave system.[20] As Davis (1981) has articulated, not only their bodies but also their reproductive capacities were the property of the slave owner. Enslaved women such as Sojourner Truth and Harriet Tubman established the analysis of the slave plantation economy through their own eyes, centering women denied bodily integrity and autonomy, economic power and political voice who, unlike White women, had no privileges in racial superiority (Cooper 1892, 1988) and unlike Black men, could lay no claim to second-class patriarchy. They created the philosophy of structural inequality that infuses the idea of intersectionality.[21]

The challenge for law is to find a way to remedy intersectional discrimination that respects synergy and that disrupts prevailing frameworks of discrimination, especially those that make certain forms of discrimination invisible, such as discrimination against fat Black women. The anti-stigma principle can help with this goal.

The anti-stigma principle

The anti-stigma principle (Solanke 2017) builds on the work of critical stigma scholars who view stigma as a social process of disempowerment. The process of stigmatization put forward by Link and Phelan (2001) lists a series of converging components: deliberate labeling of an arbitrary attribute by powerful parties in society, followed by stereotyping that separates persons with the element from others and reduces their status making them targets of discrimination. Herek (2002) lists three key characteristics of stigma: embeddedness refers to the extent to which stigma is entrenched in social norms and "common sense"; endurance relates to their longevity; and negative evaluation – the way in which stigma is used to support adverse judgment by the powerful who have means of control over the powerless (who have no access to such means). Hannem and Bruckert (2012) stress not only low social power but also low interpersonal status: stigmatization is not just a process of what people do to each other (interpersonal power) but also what society entertains and allows people to do (institutional power). It cannot be "wished away" (Plummer 1975) and thus is inescapable through individual action alone.

These ideas can be brought together in an "anti-stigma principle," and used as a logic to identify those stigmatized characteristics, attributes or statuses to be protected in antidiscrimination law. Use of the anti-stigma principle would not incorporate a completely new approach to discrimination law – immutability is, after all, a part of stigma – but on the contrary it would provide a rationale for its expansion that disrupts but does not destroy the existing framework. To retain the legal focus not all stigma should be protected – being stigmatized per se is not enough to warrant protection under anti-discrimination law – thus additional factors would have to be considered to determine which stigma warrant legal protection. Perhaps most importantly it would *de-emphasize* the ideas of innocence and blame that excludes groups suffering from discrimination, such as fat Black women, from legal protection.

The anti-stigma principle offers a simple and sustainable way to explain why law is used to prevent and protect some individuals from discrimination yet not others. It can be used to determine when a particular trait, attribute or condition is protected by anti-discrimination law, offering a practical method that is flexible without being flaccid: it allows the law to reflect upon discrimination in the twenty-first century but also to reject frivolous ideas regarding discrimination. It does this in a way that has many advantages over the current rationales for anti-discrimination law.

First, the principle takes anti-discrimination law beyond identity and individualism. Stigmas are by definition contextual: they are socially determined and maintained, and to focus on them is to prioritize social meanings (Goffman 1990). The anti-stigma principle therefore necessitates reflection upon the role of society in discrimination. It widens the view of discrimination law to situate the individual in society and analyzes the role of society in everyday discrimination. The anti-stigma principle shifts attention to social responsibility as well as individual responsibility. Restoration of the link between discrimination and society is important because it firmly anchors discrimination law: discrimination law separated from society can lose its rationale, and measures to remedy past injustice or secure future equality are easy to attack as "reverse discrimination."

Second, the anti-stigma principle highlights the idea of discrimination as the consequence of a process. There is nothing natural about stigma – a "mark" is given meaning rather than having any inherent meaning of its own. This process is a reminder that meanings are made and thus can be unmade. Third, it legitimates the use of law beyond the permanent/produced dichotomy: it includes immutable characteristics but is not limited to them. Fourth, it is flexible enough to facilitate both single dimension and intersectional discrimination: stigma can travel alone, but also in company, hence the anti-stigma principle accommodates intersectional as well as single dimension discrimination. It therefore reconstructs two aspects of the vision of anti-discrimination law – *who* it sees as well as *how* it sees. Fifth, it enables provision of legal protection for both historical and contemporary injustices, to support remedial goals as well as tackling current discrimination. Finally, as it is also sensitive to context, the anti-stigma principle can be applied in many places (for example throughout the EU) without needing to be uniform. When applied to weight, the anti-stigma principle provides a rationale for the inclusion of weight as a self-standing protected category in law.

The anti-stigma principle can be broken down into the following ten questions[22]: When applied to weight, the anti-stigma principle provides a rationale for the inclusion of weight as a self-standing protected category in law. These questions are set out below, and answered using current research from a variety of fields.

1. Is the "mark" arbitrary or does it have some meaning in and of itself?

A fat body has no meaning in and of itself – it is paradoxical that in Anglo-American societies that otherwise stress individual choice there is little recognition of a right to be fat (Tirosh 2012).

2. Is the mark used as a social label?

Fatness is a highly stigmatized condition. The higher number of people living in larger bodies has not reduced the stigma associated with "overweight" and "obesity" and the fear of being fat (Puhl and Brownell 2003) continues to exist among all age groups (Brylinsky and Moore 1994; Wardle, Volz, and Golding 1995).

3. Does this label have a long history? How embedded is it in society?

Fatness has a contested history. O' Hara (1996) suggests that in Ancient Greek societies fat women were considered beautiful; during Christianity, gluttony was considered a sin. His argument remains contested. Chrisler (2012) mentions that Magna Mater, the Earth Goddess was depicted as being short and round, with a fat waist and voluptuous breasts. Byrd (2004) points to the Statue of Liberty as evidence that there was a time when fat was a sign of health and wealth. Byrd also argues that Lillian Russell, who weighed over 200 lbs, was the "*sine qua non* of prosperous, well-heeled American beauty", admired as much for her robust appetite as her sparkling diamonds. Yet after World War II women's bodies became the targets of a new cult of thinness. The only exception to this was Black women: the ever nurturing, God-fearing full bodied trustworthy Black female "mammy" Aunt Chloe retained the ideal of the fulsome figure (Byrd 2004).

4. Can the label be "wished away"?

Fattism is so entrenched that it is easier for legislators to pass bills protecting food manufacturers rather than bills protecting from weight discrimination: by the end of 2019, only one US state – Michigan – and 6 cities have legal protection from weight discrimination. Other attempts have failed – in Utah an attempt was made in 2013 and in Massachusetts legislators have pushed for this since 2011. In contrast, at least 15 US states have adopted laws banning "obesity" lawsuits such as New Mexico"s "Right to Eat Enchiladas" Act.[23] Weight stigma has also been described as a vicious cycle: "weight stigma begets weight gain" (Tomiyama 2014, 8).

5. Is the label used to stereotype those possessing it?

There are many collective beliefs held about persons who are "overweight" and "obese." The more that behavioral understanding of weight is encouraged by official campaigns that stress healthy eating and lifestyles,[24] the greater the stereotyping. Stereotypes abound, especially for fat Black women. Shaw (2006) argues that in the USA, fatness and Blackness have a similar and complex relationship with the female body, as the twenty-first century ideal of womanhood is not only slim but also White. Thus, according to modern esthetic standards, both size and skin color undermine the viability of fat Black women to be accepted by the mainstream as women. Both characteristics (Blackness and fatness) necessitate "a degree of erasure" in order to render these women ""viable entities by Western aesthetic " (Shaw 2006, 1). Only the capacity for mothering restores the viability of the fat Black woman in the western social imaginary – her big body ""represents an overabundance of maternal resources."

6. Does the stereotype reduce the humanity of those who are its targets? Does it evoke a punitive response?

"Fattism" has been described as the "last great acceptable prejudice" (Pelling 2005; Rothblum, Miller, and Garbutt 1988). It exists in private spaces like the home[25]. as well as public spaces such as the workplace (Korn 1997; Pool 2001; Solovay 2000), healthcare and education: employers associate fat employees with higher insurance premiums, greater absenteeism, and costs for accommodations, such as new desks and chairs for their use (Chrisler 2012). Medical professionals provide different levels of care (Flint 2015). Anti-fat attitudes are prevalent even among stigmatized communities (Whitesel 2014).

7. Do these targets have low social power and low interpersonal status?

Most fat people endure everyday public disdain and are often the target of overt discrimination, open ridicule and public humiliation (Pelling 2005). Higher size reduces work opportunities and life chances. One study of over 10,000 people found that "[b]oth men and women who had been overweight were less likely to have married, had completed fewer years of education, and had lower household incomes, lower self-esteem, and higher rates of poverty that those who had not been overweight" (Gortmaker et al. 1993, 11). It might be argued that there are an increasing number of fat celebrities, such as Lizzo[26]. and Tess Holliday[27]. but as James Cordon highlighted, in Hollywood fat men are rarely cast as a romantic lead.[28]

8. Do these targets suffer discrimination as a result?

Weight discrimination is prevalent and thriving with impunity (Rothblum et al. 1990; Shinall 2015). It follows the same pattern and adverse outcomes (Wolfe 2012) as other forms of discrimination (Horner 2005) such as in employment. Fat women, such as Arazella Manuel,[29] Catherine McDermott[30]. and Joyce English[31]. were refused jobs and promotion for roles in which they had successfully demonstrated competence. Jennifer Portnick who was 5′8" tall and weighed just over 17 stone (240 lbs) was rejected for training as an exercise teacher because her fat body was considered to look unhealthy (Poole 2002).

In a poll of 300 senior leaders in major companies, more than 65% agreed that "fat people were seen as lacking in self-discipline and self-control, energy and drive" (Bento, White, and Zacur 2012; Jackson 2007).[32] Researchers have found that if hired, persons who are "obese" earn less than "non-obese" employees (Shinall 2015. Studies show that weight discrimination (Roehling 2002) is evident at every phase of the employment cycle: career counseling, selection, placement, compensation, promotion, discipline and discharge.

9. Do the targets suffer exclusion?

Fat people suffer exclusion in employment, education, healthcare, access to public accommodations, goods and services. Empirical evidence shows that there is still a "wage penalty" for being "overweight" (Judge and Cable 2011) and fat women suffer more exclusion than fat men.[33]

10. Is access to key resources blocked?

Fat people are over-represented in low-income population groups. Using poverty as a proxy for exclusion, in households with an annual income of less than 10,000, USD 33% of Black, 26% of Hispanic and 20% of White people were found to be "obese." Black and single-parent (predominantly female) households tend to fall into this lower income bracket (Critser 2003).

Conclusion

This contribution has highlighted that legal protection from fattism is not just a feminist issue, but a Black feminist issue. Fat is not a general determinant of aptitude, ability or performance yet research shows that fat individuals are subjected to discrimination in multiple areas of everyday life (Pomeranz Jennifer and Puhl 2013). I hope to have made two things clear in this article. First, as argued by Dr Susan Jebb of the Medical Research Council, "the notion of obesity simply being a product of personal over-indulgence has to be abandoned for good" (Butland et al. 2007). Second, legislators need to use the anti-stigma principle instead of immutability as the logic of anti-discrimination law.

Weight discrimination occurs with impunity because of the widespread assumption that fat is mutable (Eric and Lee 2005) – behavioral public policies that promote weight loss encourage such views that fat individuals are to blame for their size. Thus, in line with attribution theory (Corrigan et al. 2003), weight discrimination only enjoys legal protection if it is an accident of disease or disability – this is at present the surest route to a successful legal action against weight discrimination. Subsequent contributions discuss how the Americans with Disabilities Act (ADA)[34] was used by *Bonnie Cook*,[35] *Jesse Mercado*,[36] *Joseph Gimello*[37]. and *Casey Taylor*[38]. to win their cases. In Europe, *Kaltoft*[39] also used disability discrimination law.

Fat can be a disability rights issue. However, this approach to protection is no longer good enough: weight per se is not a disability – under disability law, the disabling condition must be a certified medical condition, thus outside of Washington State "obesity" *per se* does not meet the definition of a disability.[40] Entrenching protection from weight discrimination in disability law establishes fat bodies as an aberrant departure from a "normal" body. This is precisely the stereotype and stigma that courts need to address if fat people are to be protected from discrimination. Use of disability discrimination law in the long term barely improves the situation of fat people seeking protection from discrimination.

A new paradigm based on the anti-stigma principle will allow for a clearer and more consistent approach to tackling weight discrimination. The anti-stigma principle disrupts and at the same time provides a clear and effective logic to extend anti-discrimination law to prohibit discrimination on the basis of weight. The principle does not offer ready-made categories, but rather a series of questions that will guide the creation of categories in anti-discrimination law that are meaningful to the context. As weight discrimination satisfies all 10 questions posed by the anti-stigma principle, it should be added to the list of attributes protected under anti-discrimination law.

Notes

1. https://www.newsweek.com/body-beholder-181596
2. https://reykjavik.is/en/city-of-reykjaviks-human-rights-policy#6.%20Body%20build%20and%20type
3. *Reg (RJM) v Work & Pensions Secretary* [2008] UKHL 63, [2009] 1 AC 311 [5].
4. Case C-236/09 *Association belge des Consommateurs Test-Achats ASBL and Others v Conseil des Ministres.* [50] AG Opinion. See also paras 62–63, where the AG seems to challenge the modern utility of categories per se.
5. *Frontiero v Richardson* 411 US 677 (1973). See also *Weber v Aetna Casualty & Surety Co*, 406 US 164, 168 (1972); *Garcia v Gloor* 618 F.2d 264 (5 Cir. 1980), cert denied, 499 US 1113 (1981); *Caban v Mohammad*, 441 US 380 (1979); *Holland v Illinois* 493 US 474 (1990). Balog asks whether the trait has to be visible. See (Balog 2005), 545.
6. *Wolf v Walker*, 986 F. Supp. 2d 982, 1013 (W.D. Wis. 2014) the state court held that as it is "fundamental to a person's identity," sexual orientation satisfied the test of immutability.
7. *De Leon v Perry*, 975 F. Supp. 2d 632, 651 (W.D. Tex. 2014) ("[S]exual orientation is so fundamental to a person's identity that one ought not be forced to choose between one's sexual orientation and one's rights as an individual – even if one could make a choice").
8. *Bassett v Snyder*, 951 F. Supp. 2d 939, 960 (E.D. Mich. 2013) ("Even if sexual orientation were not immutable, sexual orientation is an integral part of personal identity").

9. *Golinski v US Office of Pers Mgmt*, 824 F. Supp. 2d 968, 986 (N.D. Cal. 2012), hearing en banc denied, 680 F.3d 1104 (9th Cir. 2012), appeal dismissed, 724 F.3d 1048 (9th Cir. 2013) ("[A] person's sexual orientation is so fundamental to one's identity that a person should not be required to abandon it").
10. *Griego v Oliver*, 316 P.3d 865, 884 (N.M. 2013) ("This [immutability] requirement cannot mean that the individual must be completely unable to change the characteristic. … Instead, the question is whether the characteristic is so integral to the individual's identity that, even if he or she could change it, would it be inappropriate to require him or her to do so in order to avoid discrimination?").
11. *Varnum v Brien*, 763 N.W.2d 862, 886–89 (Iowa 2009) ("[W]e agree with those courts that have held the immutability prong of the suspectness inquiry surely is satisfied when … the identifying trait is "so central to a person's identity that it would be abhorrent for government to penalize a person for refusing to change [it]."" (quoting *Watkins v US Army*, 875 F.2d 699, 703 (9th Cir. 1989)).
12. Re Marriage Cases, 183 P.3d 384, 442 (Cal. 2008) ("Because a person's sexual orientation is so integral an aspect of one's identity, it is not appropriate to require a person to repudiate or change his or her sexual orientation in order to avoid discriminatory treatment").
13. *Kerrigan v Comm'r of Pub Health*, 957 A.2d 407, 426 (Conn. 2008) ("gay persons, because they are characterized by a 'central, defining [trait] of personhood, which may be altered [if at all] only at the expense of significant damage to the individual's sense of self' are no less entitled to consideration as a suspect or quasi-suspect class than any other group that has been deemed to exhibit an immutable characteristic" (quoting *Jantz v Muci*, 759 F. Supp. 1543, 1548 (D. Kan. 1991) rev'd, 976 F.2d 623 (10th Cir. 1992).
14. *Latta v Otter*, 771 F.3d 456, 464 n.4 (9th Cir. 2014). See also *Hernandez-Montiel v INS*, 225 F.3d 1084, 1093 (9th Cir 2000).
15. *Obergefell v Wymyslo*, 962 F. Supp. 2d 968, 990 (S.D. Ohio 2013).
16. *Obergefell v Hodges*, 135 S. Ct. 2584, 2596 (2015).
17. *Degraffenreid v General Motors*, 413 F. Supp. 142 (E. D. Mo. 1976).
18. *Jefferies v Harris County Community Action Association*, 615 F. 2nd 1025 (5th 1980).
19. These claims were brought under Title VII 42 USC 2000e-2(a) (2004) that prohibits workplace discrimination.
20. Toni Morrison's *Beloved* tells the story of a slave woman who would rather kill her children than see them enslaved.
21. Further developed in (Solanke 2016).
22. These ten questions are developed in more detail in *Discrimination as Stigma* (Solanke 2017).
23. Senate Bill 291 introduced by Steve Komadina, 47th legislature, Session 1, 2005.
24. See for example the health campaign linked to COVID 19 in 2020: https://www.gov.uk/government/news/new-obesity-strategy-unveiled-as-country-urged-to-lose-weight-to-beat-coronavirus-covid-19-and-protect-the-nhs.
25. 47% of "overweight" girls and 34% of "overweight" boys reporting weight bias from families. See Puhl and Brownell (2001).
26. https://en.wikipedia.org/wiki/Lizzo
27. https://en.wikipedia.org/wiki/Tess_Holliday
28. https://www.theguardian.com/lifeandstyle/2019/apr/02/larger-actors-rarely-get-cast-as-romantic-leads-says-james-corden
29. *EEOC v Texas Bus Lines*, 923 F. Supp. 965 (S.D.TX 1996), 971.
30. *McDermott v Xerox Corp*, 102 A.D.2d 543 (1984), 544.
31. *PECO v Pennsylvania Human Relations Commission and Joyce A English*, 68 Pa. Commw. 212 (1982), 228.

32. "Obesity research: Fattism is the last bastion of employee discrimination." Personnel Today (25 October 2005), available at http://www.personneltoday.com/hr/obesity-research-fattism-is-the-last-bastion-of-employee-discrimination/.
33. For example, in the airline industry women are subject to more stringent weight standards than men. In *Frank v United Airlines* a group of female employees, who had failed to comply with United's weight requirements for women, successfully challenged the airline's weight policy. United dropped its weight policy in 1993. See also *Gerdom v Continental Airlines*, Inc, 692 F.2d 602, 605–06 (9th Cir. 1982) where customer preference was rejected by the court as justification for a weight policy discriminating against females but note *Sheela Joshi and Ors vs Indian Airlines Ltd*, Writ Petition C Nos. 12,875–83 (2006), 31 May 2007 where the Indian High Court of Delhi upheld Air India's policy as constitutional.
34. Americans with Disabilities Act (ADA) 42 USC § 12,102(2); see also *Francis v City of Meriden*, 129 F.3d 281, 286 (2d Cir. 1997). Under the ADA, a disability is defined as: (A) a physical or mental impairment that substantially limits one or more of the major life activities of such individual; (B) a record of such an impairment; or (C) being regarded as having such an impairment. See *Hazeldine v Beverage Media*, Inc, 954 F. Supp. 697 (SDNY 1997) and *Bragdon v Abbott*, 524 US 624, 638–39 (1998).
35. *Cook v State of Rhode Island Dept. of Mental Health, Retardation and Hospitals*, 783 F. Supp. 1599 (D.R.I. 1992.
36. A California jury ruled (November 9, 1990) in favor of Jesse Mercado, who was fired by the Los Angeles Times for being too fat. The Times argued that Mercado's body size was transitory or voluntary, but the jury found that he was protected by the California Fair Employment and Housing Act, which includes physical handicap and medical condition as protected categories.
37. *Gimello v Agency Rent-A-Car Systems, Inc.*, 594 A.2d 264 (NJ Super. A.D. 1991). See also *Maryland Human Relations Commission v Mass Transit Maryland*, 294 Md. 225 (Md. 1982) where a Maryland Court ruled in favor of four women (*Dorothea Goodman, Carlissa v Hawkins, Jacqueline Wilson, and Betty Wright*) who were refused jobs as bus drivers by the Maryland State Transit Authority for being over their height/weight limit. The court ruled that the Transit Authority had perceived them as disabled and that they had been unfairly discriminated against. The case took 11 years to conclude and in remedy the women were given the opportunity to reapply for the jobs.
38. *Taylor v BNSF* at https://law.justia.com/cases/federal/appellate-courts/ca9/16-35205/16-35205-2018-09-17.html; https://harvardlawreview.org/2020/03/taylor-v-burlington-northern-railroad-holdings-inc/.
39. See also in *Ireland Health Service Employee v The Health Service Executive*, December E2006-013 – Section 6(1) of the Irish Employment Equality Act (EEA) covers discrimination on the grounds of disability, including actual and potential difficulties.
40. *Torcasio v Murray*, 57 F.3d 1340, 1354 (4th Cir. 1995). Torcasio, who weighed 460 lbs and had a waist of 78 inches, sued officials at Virginia's Department of Corrections claiming that he had been treated unfairly because of his size. The court found that size alone did not qualify as a disability under the ADA.

Disclosure statement

No potential conflict of interest was reported by the author.

ORCID

Iyiola Solanke http://orcid.org/0000-0002-7068-5186

References

Andreyeva, Tatiana, Rebecca M. Puhl, and Kelly D. Brownell. 2008. "Changes in Perceived Weight Discrimination among Americans 1995–1996 through 2004–2006." *Obesity* 16:1129–34. doi: 10.1038/oby.2008.35.

Atella, Vincenzo, Noemi Pace, and Daniela Vuri. 2007. "Wages and Weight in Europe: Evidence Using Quantile Regression Model." Centre for Household, Income, Labour and Demographic Economics Working Paper 23/2007.

Austin, Regina. 1989. "Sapphire Bound!" *Wisconsin Law Review* 3:539–78.

Balog, K. 2005. "Equal Protection for Homosexuals: Why the Immutability Argument Is Necessary and How It Is Met." *Cleveland State Law Review* 53:545–72.

Baum, II, L. Charles, and William F. Ford. 2004. "The Wage Effects of Obesity: A Longitudinal Study." *Health Economics* 13:885–99. doi: 10.1002/hec.881.

Bell, Myrtle P., M. E. McLaughlin, and J. M. Sequeira. 2004. "Age, Disability, and Obesity: Similarities, Differences, and Common Threads." In *The Psychology and Management of Workplace Diversity*, edited by M. S. Stockdale and F. J. Crosby, 191–205. Malden, MA: Blackwell.

Bell, Myrtle P., and M. E. McLaughlin. 2006. "Outcomes of Appearance and Obesity in Organisations." In *Handbook of Workplace Diversity*, edited by AM Konrad, P Prasad, and J Pringle, 455–74. London: Sage.

Bento, R. F., L. F. White, and S. R. Zacur. 2012. "The Stigma of Obesity and Discrimination in Performance Appraisal: A Theoretical Model." *The International Journal of Human Resource Management* 23 (15): 3196–224. doi:10.1080/09585192.2011.637073

Bolton, Brian. 2004. "The Battle for the Armrest Reaches New Heights: The Air Carriers Access Act and the Issues Surrounding the Airlines" Policy of Requiring Obese Passengers to Purchase Additional Tickets." *Journal of Air Law and Commerce* 69:803–37.

Brylinsky, J. A., and J. C. Moore. 1994. "The Identification of Body Build Stereotypes in Young Children." *Journal Research in Personality* 28:170–81. doi: 10.1006/jrpe.1994.1014.

Butland, B., S. Jebb, P. K. McPherson, S. Thomas, J. Mardell, and V. Parry. 2007. *Tackling Obesities: Future Choices*. London: Government Office for Science. https://www.gov.uk/government/uploads/system/uploads/attachment_data/file/287937/07-1184x-tackling-obesities-future-choices-report.pdfandhttp://news.bbc.co.uk/1/hi/health/7047244.stm .

Byrd, Sayward. 2004. "Civil Rights and the "Twinkie" Tax: The 900-Pound Gorilla in the War on Obesity." *Louisiana Law Review* 65:303–85.

Cawley, John. 2004. ""The Impact of Obesity on Wages."." *The Journal of Human Resources* 392Spring:451–74. doi: 10.2307/3559022

Chrisler, Joan C. 2012. "Why Can't You Control Yourself? Fat Should Be a Feminist Issue." *Sex Roles* 66:608–16. doi: 10.1007/s11199-011-0095-1.

Clarke, Jessica A. 2015. "Against Immutability." *Yale Law Journal* 125:2–102.

Cooper, Anna J. 1892, 1988. *A Voice from the South: By A Woman from the South*. Oxford: OUP.

Corrigan, Patrick, Fred E. Markowitz, Amy Watson, David Rowan, and Mary A. Kubiak. 2003. "An Attribution Model of Public Discrimination Towards Persons with Mental Illness." *Journal of Health and Social Behaviour* 44:162–79. doi: 10.2307/1519806.

Crawford, David, and Robert W. Jeffery, eds. 2005. *Obesity Prevention and Public Health*. Oxford: OUP.

Crenshaw, Kimberlé. 1989. "Demarginalising the Intersection of Race and Sex: A Black Feminist Critique of Antidiscrimination Doctrine, Feminist Theory and Antiracial Politics." *University of Chicago Legal Forum* 1:139–67.

Critser, Greg. 2003. *Fat Land: How Americans Became the Fattest People in the World*. New York: Houghton Mifflin.

Darmer, M., and B. Katherine. 2010. "Immutability and Stigma: Towards A More Progressive Equal Protection Rights Discourse." *The American University Journal of Gender, Social Policy & the Law* 5:439–53.

Davis, Angela. 1981. *Women, Race and Class*. New York: Penguin.

Editorial. 2020. "Obesity and COVID-19: Blame Isn't a Strategy." *The Lancet* 89. https://www.thelancet.com/journals/landia/article/PIIS2213-8587(20)30274-6/fulltext#articleInformation

Eric, Oliver, J., and Taeku Lee. 2005. "Public Opinion and the Politics of America's Obesity Epidemic." *Journal of Health, Politics and Policy* 5:923–54.

Farr, Christina. 2018. "The Hidden Discrimination Against Being Fat At Work." https://www.fastcompany.com/3061210/the-hidden-discrimination-against-being-fat-at-work [Accessed August/20/2018 3:14:56 PM].

Flint, Stuart. 2015. ""Obesity Stigma: Prevalence and Impact in Healthcare."." *British Journal of Obesity* 1:14–18.

Gill, Emily R. 2014. "Beyond Immutability: Sexuality and Constitutive Choice." *The Review of Politics* 76:93–117. doi: 10.1017/S0034670513000909.

Goffman, Erving. 1990. *Stigma: Notes on the Management of Spoiled Identity*. London: Penguin.

Goldberg, Susanne B. 2004. "Equality Without Tiers." *Southern California Law Review* 77:481–582.

Gortmaker, Steven L., Aviva Must, James M. Perrin, Arthur M. Sobol, and William H. Dietz. 1993. "Social and Economic Consequences of Overweight in Adolescence and Young Adulthood." *New England Journal of Medicine* 329:1008–12. doi: 10.1056/NEJM199309303291406.

Hannem, Stacey, and Chris Bruckert, eds. 2012. *Stigma Re-visited: Re-examining the Mark*. Ottowa: University of Ottowa Press.

Hannett, Sarah. 2003. ""Equality at the Intersections: The Legislative and Judicial Failure to Tackle Multiple Discrimination." *Oxford Journal of Legal Studies* 23:65–86. doi: 10.1093/ojls/23.1.65.

Herek, Gregory M. 2002. ""Thinking about AIDS and Stigma – A Psychologist's Perspective."." *Journal of Law, Medicine and Ethics* 30:594–607. doi: 10.1111/j.1748-720X.2002.tb00428.x.

Higginbotham, B. 2003. ""A Super-sized Problem."." *International Travel Law Journal* 84–93.

Horner, Kari. 2005. "A Growing Problem: Why The Federal Government Needs To Shoulder The Burden In Protecting Workers From Weight Discrimination." *Catholic University Law Review* 54:589–626.

Hutchinson, Darren L. 2003. "Unexplainable on Grounds Other than Race: The Inversion of Privilege and Subordination in Equal Protection Jurisprudence." *University of Illinois Law Review* 3:615–700.

Jackson, Noreen. 2007. "When Bigger Isn't Always Better." *The Independent* (February):11, 2007.

Jordan, June. 1981. "Where Is the Love?" In *Civil Wars*, edited by J Jordan, 140-146. New York: Simon and Schuster.

Judge, Timothy A., and Daniel M. Cable. 2011. ""When It Comes to Pay, Do the Thin Win? the Effect of Weight on Pay for Men and Women."." *Journal of Applied Psychology* 96 (1): 95–112. doi:10.1037/a0020860

Korn, Jane B. 1997. "Fat." *Boston University Law Review* 77 (1): 25–67.

Lempert, David. 2007. "Women"s Increasing Wage Penalties from Being Overweight and Obese" US Bureau of Labour Statistics. BLS Working Paper Nr. 414.

Lien, Pei-te, Carol Hardy-Fanta, Dianne Pinderhughes, and Christine Sierra. 2008. "Expanding Categorization at the Intersection of Race and Gender: "Women of Color" as a Political Category for African American, Latina, Asian American, and American Indian Women." Paper presented at the annual meeting of the APSA 2008 Annual Meeting, Hynes Convention Center, Boston, Massachusetts, August 28, 2008. http://www.allacademic.com//meta/p_mla_apa_research_citation/2/7/9/6/8/pages279689/p279689-1.php .

Link, Bruce G., and Jo C. Phelan. 2001. "Conceptualizing Stigma." *Annual Review of Sociology* 27:363–85. doi: 10.1146/annurev.soc.27.1.363.

MacClean, Robert, and Marilyn Moon. 1980. "Health Obesity and Earnings." *American Journal of Public Health* 70 (9): 1006–09. doi:10.2105/AJPH.70.9.1006

Marcosson, Samuel A. 2001. "Constructive Immutability." *University of Pennsylvania Journal of Constitutional Law* 3 (2): 646–721.

Mason, Katherine. 2012. ""The Unequal Weight of Discrimination Gender, Body Size, and Income Inequality."." *Social Problems* 59 (3): 411–35.

Mucciaroni, Gary, and Mary L. Killian. 2004. ""Immutability, Science and Legislative Debate over Gay, Lesbian and Bisexual Rights."." *Journal of Homosexuality* 47:53–77. doi: 10.1300/J082v47n01_04.

O' Hara, M. D. 1996. ""Please Weight to Be Seated": Recognizing Obesity as a Disability to Prevent Discrimination in Public Accommodations." *Whittier Law Review* 17:895–954.

Pelling, R. 2005. ""Of Course It's Ok to Call Another Woman a Hobnob-guzzling, Lazy Lard Arse."." *Independent on Sunday* September 18, 58.

Plummer, Kenneth. 1975. *Sexual Stigma*. London: Routledge and Kegan Paul.

Pomeranz Jennifer, L., and Rebecca M. Puhl. 2013. ""Developments in the Law for Obesity."." *Obesity* 21 (3): 469–71. doi:10.1002/oby.20094

Pool, Robert. 2001. *Fat: Fighting the Obesity Epidemic*. Oxford: OUP.

Poole, Oliver. 2002. ""Victory for "Too Fat" Fitness Instructor."." *The Telegraph*, May 09. http://www.telegraph.co.uk/news/worldnews/northamerica/usa/1393682/Victory-for-too-fat-fitness-instructor.html .

Puhl, Rebecca M., and Kelly D. Brownell. 2003. ""Psychosocial Origins of Obesity Stigma: Toward Changing a Powerful and Pervasive Bias."." *Obesity Review* 4:213–27. doi: 10.1046/j.1467-789X.2003.00122.x.

Puhl, Rebecca, and Kelly Brownell. 2001. ""Bias, Discrimination, and Obesity: A Social Injustice and Public Health Priority."." *Obesity* 9 (12): 788–805. doi:10.1038/oby.2001.108

Rausch, Rebecca L. 2013. ""Health Cover(age)ing."." *Nebraska Law Review* 90:920–70.

Roehling, Mark V. 2002. "Weight Discrimination in the American Workplace: Ethical Issues and Analysis." *Journal of Business Ethics* 40 (2): 177–89. doi:10.1023/A:1020347305736

Rothblum, Esther, Carol Miller, and Barbara Garbutt. 1988. "Stereotypes of Obese Female Job Applicants." *International Journal of Eating Disorders* 7:277–83. doi: 10.1002/1098-108X(198803)7:2<277::AID-EAT2260070213>3.0.CO;2-2.

Rothblum, Esther, Pamela Brand, Carol Miller, and Helen Oetien. 1990. "The Relationship between Obesity, Employment Discrimination, and Employment-Related Victimization." *Journal of Vocational Behavior* 37 (3): 251–66. doi:10.1016/0001-8791(90)90044-3

Rubino, Francesco, R M. Puhl, D E. Cummings, R H. Eckel, D H. Ryan, J I. Mechanick, J. Nadglowski, X. Ramos Salas, P R. Schauer, D. Twenefour, *et al.* 2020. "Joint International Consensus Statement for Ending Stigma of Obesity." *Nature Medicine* 26:485–97. doi:10.1038/s41591-020-0803-x.

Saguy, Abigail C., and Kjerstin Gruys. 2010. ""Morality and Health: News Media Constructions of Overweight and Eating Disorders."." *Social Problems* 57 (2): 231–50. doi:10.1525/sp.2010.57.2.231

Scales-Trent, Judy. 1989. ""Black Women and the Constitution: Finding Our Place, Asserting Our Rights."." *Harvard Civil Rights-civil Liberties Law Review* 24:9–44.

Shapiro, Mark R. 2002. "Treading the Supreme. Court"s Murky Immutability Waters." *Gonzaga Law Review* 38:409–12.

Sharpe, Cristina. 2016. *In the Wake: On Blackness and Being*. Richmond, Virginia: Duke University Press.

Shaw, Anna E. 2006. *The Embodiment of Disobedience: Fat Black Women's Unruly Political Bodies*. Lanham, MD: Lexington Books.

Shinall, Jennifer P. 2015. "Occupational Characteristics and the Obesity Wage Penalty." Vanderbilt Law and Economics Research Paper no. 16–12. https://papers.ssrn.com/sol3/papers.cfm?abstract_id=2379575 .

Solanke, Iyiola. 2016. "A Method for Intersectional Discrimination in EU Labour Law." In *Research Handbook on EU Labour Law*, edited by Alan Bogg, Cathryn Costello, and Alan Davies, 445–73. Cheltenham: Edward Elgar.

Solanke, Iyiola. 2017. *Discrimination as Stigma*. Oxford: Hart Bloomsbury Press.

Solbes, Irene, and Ileana Enesco. 2010. "Explicit and Implicit Anti-Fat Attitudes in Children and Their Relationships with Their Body Images." *The European Journal of Obesity, Obesity Facts* 3:23–32. doi: 10.1159/000280417.

Solovay, Sondra. 2000. *Tipping the Scales of Justice*. New York: Prometheus Books.

Stein, Edward. 2011. "Sexual Orientations, Rights, and the Body: Immutability, Essentialism, and Nativism." *Social Research* 78 (2): 633–58.

Suh, Young, Rebecca M. Puhl, Sai Liu, and Frances Fleming Milici. 2014. "Support for Laws to Prohibit Weight Discrimination in the United States: Public Attitudes from 2011 to 2013." *Obesity* 22:1872–79. doi: 10.1002/oby.20750.

Tempesta, Erica, and Valerie Siebert. 2016. "Fish Is Your Friend." *Daily Mail*, March 17, 2016. http://www.dailymail.co.uk/femail/article-3497154/Fish-friend-Oprah-reveals-dieting-tips-flaunting-30lb-weight-loss-cover-O-Magazine.html .

Tirosh, Yofi. 2012. ""The Right to Be Fat."." *Yale Journal of Health Policy, Law, and Ethics* 12:264–335.

Today, Personnel. 2005. "Obesity Research: Fattism Is the Last Bastion of Employee Discrimination." http://www.personneltoday.com/hr/obesity-research-fattism-is-the-last-bastion-of-employee-discrimination/

Tomiyama, A. Janet. 2014. "Weight Stigma Is Stressful. A Review of Evidence for the Cyclic Obesity/Weight-Based Stigma Model." *Appetite* 82:8–15. doi: 10.1016/j.appet.2014.06.108.

Turner, Michelle L. 2001. "The Braided Uproar: A Defense of My Sisters Hair and an Indictment of *Rogers V American Airlines*." *Cardozo Women's Law Journal* 7:115–62.

Wardle, Jane, C Volz, and C Golding. 1995. "Social Variation in Attitudes to Obesity in Children." *International Journal of Obesity* 19:562–69.

Whitesel, Jason. 2014. *Fat Gay Men: Girth, Mirth, and the Politics of Stigma*. New York: NYU Press.

Wolfe, Bruce M. 2012. ""Presidential Address – Obesity Discrimination: What Can We Do?"." *Surgery for Obesity and Related Diseases* 8:495–500. doi: 10.1016/j.soard.2012.06.009.

Failure to launch: one-person-one-fare airline policy and the drawbacks to the disabled-by-obesity legal argument

Jen Rinaldi, Carla Rice, and Emily Lind

ABSTRACT

Since January 2009, the Canadian Transportation Agency has required domestic airlines to uphold a one-person-one-fare policy (1P1F), according to which passengers requiring additional seating due to disability – including persons found to be functionally disabled by obesity – are entitled to it without extra cost. In this article, the authors show that the jurisprudence that upholds 1P1F by design makes possible domestic airline policy and practice that impose undue obstacles for, and offend the dignity of, fat persons. Specifically, because fat flyers must prove their condition is disabling, the medical documentation they must submit discursively pathologizes their bodies. Further, the process travelers must undergo to complete and submit documentation in order to qualify for the 1P1F accommodation perpetuates, even exacerbates, their vulnerability to discriminatory treatment. The authors ultimately show that policies and processes developed to comply with Canada's 1P1F standard do pathologizing and stigmatizing work because airlines have an economic interest in holding to the "disabled by obesity" model rather than adjusting the normative geographies they produce (and profit from) on flights.

> I have a hyperawareness of my body at all times. Other people don't have to think about … their space and how much or little they're taking up, and I'm always trying not to burden someone else with my body. (Bias and Evans 2016)

Fat activist and artist Stacy Bias, in collaboration with fat studies scholar Bethan Evans, launched the open access animated documentary *Flying While Fat* in December 2016. The video showcased live recordings from in-depth interviews, wherein fat-identified participants related their experiences of air travel. They described encounters with hostile passengers assigned seats beside them: how some yelled at them or flight attendants, refused to sit or demanded to be moved, or slammed down armrests on their bodies. When reflecting on this hostility, the people interviewed considered the conditions of airline travel that engender an entitlement to space, one noting, "the space itself is so commodified;" another saying, "everyone is fully aware of how much money they spent for those cubic inches" (Bias and Evans 2016). The interior specifications of aircrafts are not designed to provide adequate comfortable space per person, and fat persons feel this reality when they cram themselves into their seats, or encounter vitriol and violence for taking up space.

Canadian regulatory bodies developed mechanisms to adjust to these spatial conditions. Effective January 2009, the Canadian Transportation Agency (CTA) circulated a Memorandum that required several prominent domestic airlines to uphold a one-person-one-fare standard (1P1F), according to which passengers requiring additional seating due to disability – either for their personal attendant, for service animal support, or for themselves, "including those determined to be functionally disabled by obesity" – are entitled to it without extra cost[1] (Canadian Transportation Agency 2014). While the Memorandum does not explicitly elaborate on how airline passengers specifically would qualify for 1P1F, implementation of this standard coincided with a Federal Court (FC) decision that found Linda McKay-Panos was "disabled by obesity" and should not have to face undue obstacles by being forced to pay more than non-disabled persons pay in order to fly (McKay-Panos v Air Canada 2006). The application of 1P1F to fat passengers can thus be interpreted through the "disabled by obesity" standard explained in the *McKay-Panos* ruling.

The 1P1F standard marks an improvement for fat persons flying across Canada, but there are adverse implications to fatness manifesting in law in association with disability, particularly given that the *McKay-Panos* decision found that not all fat persons could claim to be disabled. In this article, we show that the jurisprudence that upholds 1P1F by design makes possible domestic airline policy and practice that impose undue obstacles for, and offend the dignity of, fat persons. Specifically, we show through an analysis of domestic tariffs that because fat passengers must prove their condition is disabling, the medical documentation they must submit discursively pathologizes their bodies. Further, through phone calls paid to domestic airlines to ask about the process, we found that the process passengers must undergo to complete and submit documentation in order to qualify for the 1P1F accommodation perpetuates, even exacerbates, their vulnerability to discriminatory treatment. Ultimately, we argue that policies and processes developed to comply with Canada's 1P1F standard do pathologizing and stigmatizing work because airlines have an economic interest in holding to the "disabled by obesity" model rather than adjusting the normative geographies they produce (and profit from) on flights.

The "disabled by obesity" standard

Canada's one-person-one-fare standard developed in a decision rendered by the Canadian Transportation Agency (hereafter called the Agency). As a quasi-juridical body, the Agency has regulatory, investigatory, and judicial powers granted under its enabling statute, the *Canada Transportation Act* (CTA) (1996). Agency decisions can be appealed in Federal Court to review the application of the law. Duties as listed under the CTA, specifically section 172(2), include determining whether there is any "undue obstacle to the mobility of persons with disabilities" and offering remedy by way of monetary awards and/or performance orders. (Canada Transportation Act 1996; Williams 2009).

In 2008 the Agency circulated a key Memorandum of Fact and Law that expanded the application of s. 172(2) (Luther 2010). The Memorandum was due to Eric Norman and Joanne Neubauer (who were not fat but physically disabled) working with the Council of Canadians with Disabilities to file a complaint with the Agency against three Canadian airlines: Air Canada, WestJet, and Air Canada Jazz (Canadian Transportation Agency Decision 2008). The class alleged that these airlines' pricing policies transgressed s. 172(2) of the CTA by charging disabled persons fares for second seats. The policies constituted an undue obstacle to the mobility of disabled persons. The complaint resulted in the Agency ruling in accordance with s. 172(2) of the CTA that pricing policies that impose one fare per seat constitute an undue obstacle for disabled persons. The corrective Memorandum applied to the representative airlines' domestic flights, particularly impacting Canada's largest domestic passenger airlines Air Canada and WestJet[2] (Associated Press 2008) and Delta Air Lines Inc. v Lukacs (2018). Specifically, it ordered the three airlines to modify their policies for domestic flights in accordance with a one-person-one-fare standard, effective January 2009 (Canadian Transportation Agency Decision 2008). According to the 1P1F rule, the implicated airlines cannot charge passengers for a second seat when those passengers are disabled and require a second seat for accommodation purposes.

While the 1P1F rule was designed to apply to disability broadly, "obese" passengers qualify for 1P1F thanks to the interpretation of "obesity" found in the *McKay-Panos* decision. Linda McKay-Panos was described in her lawsuit as "morbidly obese" – a condition attributed to Stein-Leventhal syndrome (McKay-Panos v Air Canada 2006, para 3). In June 1997, she contacted Air Canada to book a return flight from Calgary to Ottawa, with a layover in Toronto. She identified her weight and requested two economy seats or one business class seat in case a single economy seat would not accommodate her size (McKay-Panos v Air Canada 2006). She was informed there was no need to purchase two seats, and her request was "met with several off-hand remarks and laughter" (McKay-Panos v Air Canada 2006, para 5). She described the Calgary to Toronto flight as follows: "she could barely force herself into her seat. The passenger beside her could not access his tray because her hips spread onto his armrest. The flight attendants bumped into her with their serving carts" (McKay-Panos v Air Canada 2006, para 6). A flight attendant gave her a vacant business class seat on her flight from Toronto to Ottawa, a gesture McKay-Panos identifies as "the only act of human dignity that she experienced during her trip" (McKay-Panos v Air Canada 2006, para 7). Two days prior to her return flight out of Ottawa, she called Air Canada to request assistance. She was informed that her flights to home were overbooked, but she could purchase a business class seat for the Toronto to Calgary segment for 972 USD. She would not be credited for the economy seat she had already purchased. She purchased the ticket, and upon her return home, she filed a complaint for the cost and for discourteous treatment, on the grounds that the airline had failed in their duty to accommodate her under s. 172(2) of the CTA (McKay-Panos v Air Canada 2006).

McKay-Panos's complaint raised complications around whether "obesity" constitutes a disability according to the language of the CTA. A preliminary review of her complaint made clear a decision in this matter would significantly impact the federal transportation network; a three-member panel thus consulted widely on the jurisdictional issues raised, resulting in "the Calgary decision" before returning to its application to McKay-Panos's complaint (Canadian Transportation Agency Decision 2001). On the advice of experts, the panel adopted the World Health Organization's model of disability titled ICF, for "International Classification of Functioning" (McKay-Panos v Air Canada 2006, para 16). According to the ICF model: "some obese persons had impairments and experienced activity limitations and participation restrictions; as such, they were disabled" (Luther 2010, 176). This definition meant that "obesity, *per se*, was not a disability for the purposes of the CTA" (176). Whether "obesity" constituted a disability would need to be determined on a case-by-case basis. In *McKay-Panos*, the same panel responsible for the Calgary decision dismissed her complaint on the grounds that she had inappropriately applied the ICF model to establish her "obesity" as a disability. The three-step analysis for determining whether s. 172(2) was satisfied required that a complainant show that 1) they are disabled, 2) they encountered an obstacle, and 3) the obstacle was undue (Williams 2009). In a split decision, the panel determined that McKay-Panos claimed to be disabled by the obstacle itself – her seating. Because "obesity *per se*" is not a disability, her disability must be established before she can claim she encountered an obstacle. According to Avery Williams's critique of these back-to-back decisions: "The Calgary decision used sweeping language; created a general, open-ended test for obesity-disability; and elevated transportation access to a basic human right. Contrast that with the limiting language, backpedaling, and reversion to a technicality in the subsequent decision" (670).

In McKay-Panos's appeal, the Federal Court bench set aside the original decision and referred the issue back to the Agency to re-assess (McKay-Panos v Air Canada 2006). As noted in the FC decision, "the majority [of the Agency panel] refused to take into account the limitation the appellant identified: the seat" (para 34). The FC acknowledged that McKay-Panos had explained that the requirement of occupying a single economy seat imposed an activity limitation and "as a result, she suffered what she described as terrible pain" *McKay-Panos v Air Canada* (para 35). The Agency was found correct in asserting that "the determination of whether a person is disabled must be based on the CTA," but erred "when it held that the CTA directs that the obstacle (i.e. the seat) cannot be considered in making this determination" (McKay-Panos v Air Canada 2006). Having the complaint referred back to the Agency to re-litigate according to these parameters was promising for McKay-Panos herself, but the FC upheld the Calgary decision's premise that "obesity *per se*" should not qualify for accommodation support.

The 1P1F standard did not directly derive from McKay-Panos's complaint, or more generally from a complaint involving fat passengers, and so it did not directly address what it means to be "disabled by obesity" (Williams 2009). How the 1P1F Memorandum applies to fat airline passengers is contingent on the CTA Calgary decision limiting who qualifies as "disabled by obesity," and its refinement in *McKay-Panos.* In effect, the 1P1F rule combined with the call to assess accommodation requests on a case-by-case basis has resulted in the institutionalization of complicated assessment regimes that re-inscribe weight discrimination.

Implications for fat airline passengers

The notion that fat passengers have been rendered "disabled by obesity" is a limited framework for understanding why a passenger may require an extra seat to fly safely. While the language of disability opens up a protocol for accommodating non-normative bodies and travel needs, the functional need of an "obese" body is to sit in a seat that fits. Airlines do not demonstrate that their assessments take into consideration the passenger's ability or accommodation needs to board or exit the aircraft, use the washroom facilities, consume any food or beverages on board, or use assistive devices. The only function passengers are noted as disabled from doing is sitting in their assigned seat when there is another passenger seated next to them.

The accommodation is limited in scope when tied solely to seat width, and seat width itself remains unregulated, which means airlines are incentivized to prioritize their economic interests over passengers' accommodation needs.

There are seats in nearly every airplane that are larger and more flexibly designed: those found in areas of the aircraft labeled business, elite, executive, plus, premium, premium economy, and signature, among other names. There is a positive relationship between the seat size and the cost of a ticket in commercial air travel.[3] The most expensive seats in an airplane are also the largest. Airlines thus have an economic incentive to sell wide seats for higher prices rather than reserve them for large bodies. Airlines are doubly incentivized to purchase and have designed aircraft that carry as many passengers as possible, thereby putting downward pressure on seat sizes across the sector. For these reasons, the average width for higher priced seats on Canadian domestic flights is 20.6 inches, with the widest seat – on an Air Canada plane – measuring 24 inches.[4] By contrast, the standard seat width in economy cabins is 17 inches; and in the absence of seat regulation, that standard reflects a contraction of seat width from a previous 18-inch minimum, to fit more seats per row (Deveau 2013).

The frameworks for securing extra seating as an accommodation thus err in only paying heed to seat width considering how varied seat width can be: a passenger can be functionally limited on one aircraft but not another, or in economy but not business class. This suggests that a fat passenger is disabled not by "obesity," but by aircraft specifications and the economic motivations informing those specifications. Activists advocating for disability justice and scholars studying disability have explored in detail how socio-economic conditions shape space in ways that exclude non-normative bodies and produce material impacts on those bodies that do not fit (Erevelles 2011; Garland-Thomson 2011). We mean to suggest that the Agency did not necessarily err when finding there is a relationship between fatness and disability; only that the articulation of this relationship misses how fat and disabled persons have been excluded and impacted, and how they should be accommodated.

Broadly, as Bias and Evans document in their own research, fat passengers experience a range of material impacts when relegated to a single seat (Bias and Evans 2016). These impacts include the physical discomfort that accompanies bodily contortions and pressing into and against spaces that offer a poor fit (and here we reference not only seats but also aircraft aisle ways and washrooms). Passengers also risk their health and safety flying in a single small seat without accommodation, particularly blood clotting, hypertension, and dehydration if they are afraid or unable to move about the aircraft. They face the possibility of discrimination through the duration of flights and while booking, from airline staff and fellow passengers. They face the risk of physical assault when a fellow passenger believes they or their fat encroaches upon "entitled" seat space. These risks taken together may deter fat persons from flying at all, which affects their capacities for social participation – on holiday with family and friends, and travel for work and leisure. These risks remain real for passengers applying for accommodations under 1P1F, and in what follows we show how the 1P1F regime itself produces adverse impacts.

Medical documentation and discursive pathology

In order to qualify for a second seat without cost on Canadian domestic flights, passengers must prove they are "disabled by obesity" via documentation that the airline provides or a process that the airline has established[5] (Canadian Transportation Agency Decision 2008). The procedures for requesting accommodation are outlined in domestic tariffs – terms and conditions that all domestic air carriers are obligated by law to make public. We reviewed the domestic tariffs for Canadian air carriers that operate scheduled passenger travel, excluding those that explicitly operate light aircraft (29 seats or fewer).[6] Several regional airlines do not explicitly reference "obesity" in their tariffs.[7] They include sections on accommodating disability (typically referencing medical clearance and advance notice). The CTA has interpreted disability to include "obesity" (on a case-by-case basis), so it would stand to reason that "obesity" can be read into these sections. But in the absence of explicit reference to the term, these airlines have no established framework to apply for extra seating, or documentation to secure extra seating. Several tariffs (including those issued by Canada's top two airlines, Air Canada and WestJet) explicitly reference 1P1F, or indicate that persons requiring a second seat as an accommodation are entitled to that seating free of charge, though the regional airlines that use this language in their tariffs provide a service number to make arrangements rather than an application form.[8] In what follows, we review the paperwork that the major and some regional airlines use to implement 1P1F. We consider the implications to their discursive framings of "disabled by obesity," particularly the yielding of authority to a medical practitioner, the language used to describe the fat passenger, and the processes and units of measurement by which size is medicalized[9] (Conrad 2007; Hayes and Hannold 2007).

The data collected for our analysis entail medical documentation provided by Air Canada, WestJet, and select independent regional airlines. Air Canada is Canada's national, flag-carrying airline founded in 1937, with subsidiaries Air Canada Express (a regional airline founded in 2011 after Air Canada Jazz was retired) and Air Canada Rouge (a budget airline founded in 2012). Air Canada provides a *Fitness for Air Travel* form that includes *Section 3 – Extra Seating by Reason of Obesity* (Advance Notice and Medical Approval 2017). WestJet Airlines is Canada's second-largest Canadian airline, founded in 1996. Its subsidiaries include WestJet Encore, which has operated regional flights on small-range aircrafts since 2013; WestJet Link, which has operated feeder flights in British Columbia and Alberta since 2017; and Swoop, which has operated low-cost flights since 2018.[10] WestJet provides a medical form without a title, marked as version 3 (Seating Accommodation n.d.).

Regional passenger airlines independent of Air Canada and WestJet do not all provide medical documentation templates to complete or indication of accommodation procedures on their websites. Our data pool includes the airlines that provide forms, but that list is limited and comes with caveats. Canadian North, founded in 1998 with headquarters at the Edmonton Airport, operates flights to northern territories. The airline provides a faxable form titled *Incapacitated Passenger's Handling Advice* (Special Needs 2009). Porter Airlines, founded in 2006 with headquarters at Billy Bishop Toronto City Airport, offers a form titled *Request for Additional Seating for Self for Reasons of Disability (Obesity)* that explicitly references 1P1F (Disability Assistance 2018). Running budget flights since 2005 with operating bases at two Toronto airports, Sunwing Airlines offers a *Special Services Request Form* that includes a section for "obese passengers," though this form does not enact a 1P1F standard (Special Assistance 2019).

Excluding Sunwing (which can be completed entirely by passengers), airlines' medical forms include portions to be completed by passengers, and portions to be completed by medical practitioners; and medical forms are reviewed by the airlines' resident medical departments before extra seating is approved.[11] The relevant portion of the Air Canada form (Section 3) must be completed by the passenger's attending physician in the case of a first assessment, but renewals can be completed by occupational therapists, physiotherapists, or nurse practitioners (Advance Notice and Medical Approval 2017). Beyond Air Canada's exception for renewals, airlines otherwise require that medical forms be completed by attending physicians who can provide their contact information and license numbers. Canadian North requires a signed declaration that the passenger authorizes their physician to deliver the form with up-to-date information, and WestJet and Porter require that the passenger consent and agree to their physician providing and discussing the medical information requested. WestJet extends this consent to authorizing the airline medical department's access to discussing "information relevant to [the applicant's] fitness to fly" with other medical professionals or support organizations as identified by the attending physician (Seating Accommodation n.d.). These forms thus locate authority for determining whether the passenger is "obese" and whether their "obesity is disabling" entirely with medical practitioners. The discussions that passenger declarations authorize between attending physicians and airline medical departments diminish passengers' agency by circumventing their participation in decision-making processes related to their applications.

How the applicant is characterized fluctuates per form, and per page. On the forms supplied by Air Canada, Canadian North, and Porter Airlines, the term *passenger* is used in the sections that the passenger themselves complete, and the term *patient* is used in the sections that the medical practitioner completes. WestJet uses the term *patient* throughout its form, with the exception of the *Guest information section* – "to be completed by guest/patient" (Seating Accommodation n.d.). This linguistic shift ostensibly reflects the shifts in form addressees, but also does discursive work, for *patient* reconstitutes the fat subject who may only be brought in contact with medical authorities for the purpose of flying, rather than to treat a medical need. That is, a passenger requiring an accommodation becomes a patient through the completion of these forms. Related, *obesity* – a term contested in critical obesity and fat studies scholarship for its medical and derogatory connotations – is consistently used across documentation, which signals the commitment airlines are making to medicalizing the condition they are accommodating (Ellison, McPhail, and Mitchinson 2016; Kirkland 2018; Saguy 2014). The forms' language follows the legal terminology "disabled by obesity," that standard that must be met in order to qualify for accommodation support; but in line with the CTA's interpretation of the standard in the Calgary decision, "disabled by obesity" only needs to mean that a person's size exceeds an aircraft's seat width, insofar as the seat constitutes an undue obstacle.

The medicalization of size is further reinforced in forms' units of measurement and instructions to measure. The Air Canada form asks for the applicant's weight and height, confirmation of Body Mass Index (a calculation based on weight and height), and surface measurement (Advance Notice and Medical Approval 2017). A person's surface measurement, the form instructs, "should be calculated by measuring the distance between the extreme widest projection points of the patient when seated" (5). The patient sits on a papered-over examination table and the medical practitioner marks two points on the paper by "rest[ing] a ruler or straightedge" on each side of the patient's posterior. The distance between the two markings – Point A to Point B – constitutes the surface measurement. Canadian North also asks for a BMI and provides comparable instructions on finding surface measurement (Special Needs 2009). While BMI may determine whether a person is medically classified as "obese," the measure is irrelevant to seat size (Ernsberger 2012; Nuttall 2015). Surface measurement appears to be the measure most closely related to seat width, though the measurement method is strikingly degrading. WestJet asks for "the patient's circumference (taken while standing)," including height, weight, "waist at umbilicus," and "maximum girth of hips above gluteal fold" (Seating Accommodation n.d.). These requirements are especially arbitrary, obscure, and potentially humiliating given that physicians must obtain them.

The submission process and stigmatization

The submission process itself is fraught in how it downloads responsibility for managing the process onto individual passengers who must act as their own advocates in order to secure accommodations; and how it creates procedural and financial roadblocks to completing applications. To investigate submission processes implemented by four Canadian airlines, we reviewed online information about 1P1F accommodations, and then we generated a list of outstanding questions. We sought answers to our queries by contacting medical, special service, or customer service representatives of the airlines we targeted via telephone and e-mail contact information provided online. Identifying as a fat passenger seeking clarity about the 1P1F application and adjudication process, each of the authors of this article contacted at least one airline representative in the relevant accommodations/support/assistance department between November 29 and December 7, 2018 (Rinaldi contacted Air Canada, Rice contacted WestJet and Swoop, and Lind contacted Porter Airlines). We followed similar scripts: we introduced ourselves, explained that we needed to book travel for work, and identified that we might qualify for a second seat without cost if we did not fit into standard economy seat sizes. We took detailed notes (or archived e-mails) of the representative's responses to our queries.

Though not comprehensive, we believe our research in this section provides a snapshot of how airlines handle 1P1F. Our list of four contacts includes Canada's two largest airlines (Air Canada and WestJet), and two regional airlines: Porter explicitly references 1P1F in its medical form; and Swoop is a WestJet property, which raised questions for us around whether WestJet imposes a systematized implementation strategy of 1P1F across its properties. That is, while Air Canada properties direct passengers to a standard *Fitness for Air Travel* form and provide a centralized submission process, and other WestJet properties with the word *WestJet* in their names take the same approach, Swoop offers passengers an adapted version of WestJet's submission form and instructs passengers to submit forms and inquiries to Swoop-specific contact information.

Though the specific processes of each airline varied, we found that all obfuscate the steps that fat passengers must take to be considered for additional seating due to "disabling obesity," impose bureaucratic hurdles and financial obstacles on passengers who must navigate a maze of sometimes erroneous online and telephone information sources to decipher the process, and offer confusing sets of instructions that passengers must follow precisely to ensure their accommodation request is reviewed by airline medical personnel. Applicants must subject themselves to this humiliating process with a considerable outlay of their own time, and with no guarantees that they will secure a second no-cost seat.

A majority of representatives of the airlines contacted were tentative and unsure about their company's 1P1F accommodation policy and procedure, saying many times over that they "never had to handle a request like this" (Porter) or that they "never helped with a matter like this before" (Air Canada). This response alone suggests that most fat passengers in Canada either 1) do not know about the rule; or 2) may feel too humiliated by the process to subject themselves to it. Perhaps the most egregious experience we had was with low-cost Swoop, which after placing Rice on hold for almost 60 minutes, transferred her to a medical support representative who explained that Swoop's 1P1F policy only allowed people to "book and pay for two seats" – placing Swoop's policy, or at least this representative's interpretation of it, at odds with the actual 1P1F standard. According to the agent, Swoop's policy is really one person two fares, and only so long as a customer's application for extra seating is approved. Without completing and submitting the medical form and following up with Swoop for booking assistance, the agent explained, customers are not guaranteed side-by-side seats.

Also significant is that in all of these cases, passengers must purchase a plane ticket prior to submitting their medical form requesting extra seating, even though submitting this form does not guarantee that the airline will approve their request. Using disclaimers posted online and on the medical forms, airlines advise that passengers are responsible for any added costs associated with filling out the forms, which in Canada are called third-party medical forms – and are not covered by national health insurance. Canadian federal and provincial medical associations provide a range of costs to patients filling out third party medical forms; using these as guides, we estimate that a passenger would have to pay anywhere between 25 and 40 CAD to have their physicians complete a fit for air travel form (see Appendix A). In probing airline representatives, we learned that no airline would reimburse passengers for this out-of-pocket expense even if an application for extra seating was denied. Representatives also admitted that if an application was not approved and a passenger did not (or perhaps could not) fly, then that passenger would incur all additional cancellation fees. The Swoop representative advised that it was essential that physicians checked off "NA" for *not applicable* in all the sections of their form, even those sections that did not apply to the passenger; otherwise, the form might be considered incomplete and might not be processed.

Our calls show that potential passengers face these economic barriers without the guarantee they will be accommodated. Not only do they pay medical form fees that will not be reimbursed regardless of whether or not they qualify for a second seat under 1P1F, but they also book flights before accommodations are approved. When a passenger is not found to be "disabled by obesity," their already-purchased seat falls under airlines' cancellation policies. Their choice is to incur cancellation costs, or to compromise their comfort and safety (outlined in "Implications for Fat Airline Passengers") by flying without the accommodation of a second seat. Remember that when McKay-Panos was denied accommodation support, she purchased business class seating, and could not cancel her original economy seat booking.

All the airlines we contacted further advised us to submit our forms as far in advance of travel as possible to ensure that the paperwork would be processed in time for our departure date. Despite the form instructing physicians to submit applicant medical forms 48 hours before the flight, the Air Canada agent stressed and repeated that applicants should submit their medical forms at least 48–72 hours in advance of travel or as soon as possible beforehand. In contrast, Porter required applicants to submit their form at least 48 hours before their scheduled flight; WestJet requested a minimum of five business days to process applications; and Swoop required the paperwork to be submitted at least 15 days in advance of flying. After a form was submitted and approved, the Porter agent admitted that it would stay on file under a passenger's name for three months only, so if that passenger traveled as little as four months later, they would have to go through the whole process again. The Swoop agent advised that their form was good for up to one year. The Air Canada form is subject to renewal in two years (or shorter if the passenger's health status changes in that timeframe). WestJet might grant approval for up to three years; the agent qualified, though, that approval could be given for a year or less depending on a passenger's specific health condition.

As a result of this research, we found that there seems to be no way of anticipating how fat one must be in order to get approval for additional seating – in other words, no way of figuring out specific airline criteria for granting or withholding extra seat space. For example, the Porter representative indicated that no guidelines have been given to Porter agents to advise passengers about the metrics that Porter uses to determine which bodies are considered small enough to fit in its economy-sized seats and which are categorized as big enough to require accommodation. In an e-mail exchange with WestJet's "Meddesk" on their "fit to fly" evaluation criteria, a company representative wrote that, '[t]he criteria used to determine [if a passenger qualifies for extra seating] is based on measurements that are inputted into a mathematical algorithm to determine whether one seat or two is required." However, no information was forthcoming about the kinds of "measurements" inputted or the "mathematical algorithm" used to determine the seating a passenger might require. By obfuscating how they decide who qualifies for extra space under the 1P1F standard, companies can change the dimensions (width, depth, pitch) of economy-sized seats at will to maximize profits; implement pathologizing, extractive (in terms of both time and money), and confusing procedures that deter customers from applying for extra space; for those fat passengers who do manage to apply for accommodation, decline applications by employing opaque formulas that constrain fat people to squeeze their bodies into economy-sized seats, and endure vitriol and violence from neighboring passengers; and finally, make it difficult, if not impossible, for passengers to appeal decisions. Mystification of the metrics used to determine whether or not a passenger qualifies for extra space leaves us to draw one conclusion about airline implementation of the 1P1F policy: that fat people need not apply.

Conclusion

The paperwork and processes for implementing 1P1F – for their inconvenience, humiliation, and social violence – function to deter passengers from making accommodation claims. Whether a passenger is "disabled by obesity" fluctuates wildly, contingent on context and economic privilege. This means that "disabled by obesity" simply does not work as an effective threshold for determining whether an airline passenger qualifies for accommodation support. We are left to conclude that the 1P1F policy fails fat passengers by resting on a "disabled by obesity" determination, because the problem is not the passenger's body. By resting on 1P1F, the Canadian Transportation Agency has failed to prevent discrimination against fat passengers by regulating airlines.

Notes

1. Obesity is the language used in law. The term is in scare quotes in accordance with this journal's formatting guidelines.
2. International flights do not fall within the Memorandum's purview; nor do charter carriers, but the Agency has expressed the hope that if major airlines implement 1P1F the standard may spread across Canada's airline industry. The Memorandum, specifically its application outside domestic flights, is being put to the test in the ongoing *Delta Air Lines Inc. v Lukacs*, (2018) SCC 2.
3. In our review of aircraft interior specifications, we found that higher priced cabins in some aircraft (called "premium" cabins in Air Canada Rouge, Porter, and Swoop aircraft, and "plus" cabins in WestJet Encore aircraft) provide greater seat pitch for extra legroom, but not greater seat width compared to economy cabin seats. Otherwise, the key feature that distinguishes economy from higher priced cabins across Canadian airlines is seat width.
4. Air Canada makes the interior specifications for their fleet, including seat width, publicly available. Other airlines are not forthcoming around seat width in their interior specs, so we consulted with a crowd-sourced guide Seat Guru, which identifies seat widths for the fleets of large airlines. While determining the seat widths of regional airline fleets proved to be a more difficult feat via these methods, we did find that

regional and major airlines purchased aircraft from the same manufacturers, and typically hold aircraft models in common.

5. The Canadian Transportation Agency Decision No. 6-AT-A-2008 only applies to the airlines represented in the lawsuit, but domestic airlines tend to implement a 1P1F standard to avoid potential lawsuits.
6. Light aircraft includes seaplanes, helicopters, medivacs, charters, and cargo carriers. Domestic tariffs treat seating for 29 vs 30 passengers as a dividing line when stipulating terms and conditions for aircrafts.
7. Specifically: Air Inuit, Air North Yukon, Flair Airlines, Northstar Air, Pacific Coastal Airlines, Perimeter Aviation, Transwest Air, Wasaya Airlines, and WestWing Aviation. Porter Airlines also lacks explicit reference to "obesity" in their domestic tariffs, but its accommodation application process uses a medical form that references 1P1F.
8. Air Canada (Section 4aii), Air Creebec (Rule 71), and Canadian North (Rule 21) explicitly identify that they provide extra seating as an accommodation at no cost. Calm Air (Rule 17), Provincial Airlines (Rule 25), and WestJet (Rule 71) call this type of accommodation a One Person One Fare program.
9. Medicalization refers to processes by which an embodied difference (eg, disability) or bodily process (eg, pregnancy) is made sense of solely through a medical lens. Medicalization props up medical authorities as experts over the bodies of marginalized populations.
10. WestJet Link is the result of an agreement with Pacific Coastal Airlines, a smaller Canadian airline that operates scheduled, charter, and cargo flights in British Columbia and Alberta. While the Pacific Coastal Airline tariffs do not refer to obesity in their section on accommodating disability, and their website does not offer a medical form to complete in order to qualify for a second no-cost seat, potential passengers book WestJet Link flights through WestJet. They would thus have access to the WestJet medical form. Swoop provides its own medical form on their website; it is identical in all but font color to the WestJet medical form.
11. The Sunwing form asks for passengers to select the box "do you require the use of an additional seat?" and follows the question with the parenthetical "(Additional cost)," which indicates that the accommodation of extra seating is only supplied at the expense of the passenger.

Disclosure statement

No potential conflict of interest was reported by the authors.

ORCID

Jen Rinaldi http://orcid.org/0000-0003-0545-3941
Carla Rice http://orcid.org/0000-0001-7490-8749

References

Legislation

Canada Transportation Act, SC 1996, c 10.

Jurisprudence

Canadian Transportation Agency Decision No. 646-AT-A-2001.
Canadian Transportation Agency Decision No. 6-AT-A-2008.
Delta Air Lines Inc. v Lukacs. 2018. SCC 2.
McKay-Panos v Air Canada and The Canadian Transportation Agency. 2006. FCA 8.

Secondary Material: Scholarly Sources

Conrad, Peter. 2007. *The Medicalization of Society: On the Transformation of Human Conditions into Trea' Disorders*. Baltimore: Johns Hopkins University Press.
Ellison, Jenny, Deborah McPhail, and Wendy Mitchinson. 2016. "Introduction: Obesity in Canada." In *Obesity in Canada: Critical Perspectives*, edited by Jenny Ellison, Deborah McPhail, and Wendy Mitchinson. Toronto: UT Press. p.3-28.

Erevelles, Nirmala. 2011. *Disability and Difference in Global Contexts: Enabling a Transformative Body Politic.* New York: Palgrave Macmillan.
Ernsberger, Paul. 2012. "BMI, Body Build, Body Fatness, and Health Risks." *Fat Studies* 1 (1):6. doi:10.1080/21604851.2012.627788.
Garland-Thomson, Rosemarie. 2011. "Misfits: A Feminist Materialist Disability Concept."*Hypatia* 26 (3):591. doi:10.1111/j.1527-2001.2011.01206.x.
Hayes, Jeanne, and Elizabeth Hannold. 2007. "The Road to Empowerment: A Historical Perspective on the Medicalization of Disability." *Journal of Health and Human Services Administration* 30:352.
Kirkland, Anna. 2018. *Fat Rights: Dilemmas of Difference and Personhood.* New York: NYU Press.
Luther, Emily. 2010. "Justice for All Shapes and Sizes: Combatting Weight Discrimination in Canada." *Alberta Law Review* 48 (1):167. doi:10.29173/alr167.
Nuttall, Frank. 2015. "Body Mass Index: Obesity, BMI, and Health: A Critical Review" *Nutrition Today* 50 (3):117. doi:10.1097/NT.0000000000000092.
Saguy, Abigail C. 2014. *What's Wrong with Fat?* Cambridge: Oxford University Press.
Williams, Avery. 2009. "Obesity, Canada's One Passenger Fare Rule and the Potential Effects on the U.S. Commercial Airline Industry" *Journal of Air Law and Commerce* 74:663.

Secondary Material: Web Sources

Associated Press. "One-person, One-fare on Canadian Airlines." *NBC News*, January 10, 2008. http://www.nbcnews.com/id/22599803/ns/travel-news/t/one-person-one-fare-canadian-airlines/#.W8zq0flReUk.
Bias, Stacy, and Bethan Evans. "Flying While Fat." *Youtube*. Accessed December 2016. https://www.youtube.com/watch?v=Eoiml0Co50Y.
Canadian Transportation Agency. "Highlights of One-person-one-fare Policy Decision." *CTA*. Accessed May 12, 2014. https://otc-cta.gc.ca/eng/content/highlights-one-person-one-fare-policy-decision.
Deveau, Scott. "The Great Seat Squeeze: How Airlines are Trying to Pack More People on a Plane without Anybody Knowing." *Financial Post*, March 23, 2013. https://business.financialpost.com/transportation/the-great-seat-squeeze-how-to-pack-more-people-on-a-plane-without-anybody-knowing.

Secondary Material: Forms

"Advance Notice and Medical Approval". *Air Canada*. Accessed September 2017. https://www.aircanada.com/ca/en/aco/home/plan/medical-mobility/advance-notice-and-medical-approval.html.
"Disability Assistance". *Porter*. Accessed January 2018. https://www.flyporter.com/en-ca/travel-information/disability-assistance.
"Seating Accommodation". n.d.. *WestJet*. https://www.westjet.com/en-ca/travel-info/special-needs/seating.
"Special Assistance". 2019. *Sunwing*. https://www.sunwing.ca/pages/en/sunwing-airlines/special-assistance.
"Special Needs". *Canadian North*. Accessed July 31, 2009. https://www.canadiannorth.com/info/special-needs.

OPEN ACCESS

Crossroad between the right to health and the right to be fat

Friedrich Schorb

ABSTRACT

The right to health has been little more than a patchwork of international treaties and covenants with mostly symbolic value. More recently though, attempts to define the right to health have become more concrete and related to specific topics such as the prevention of over- and malnutrition as well as fatness. The right to health in this context is meant to create an environment that makes it less likely to consume foods considered to be unhealthy and fattening. The measures applied here are mostly restrictive. In this paper, two main lines of critique are presented with regard to the right to health in the context of nutrition and fatness – a libertarian and a social justice argument. Based on this reasoning, the right to health as articulated in this context is criticized as incompatible with the right to be fat. On the other hand, it will be argued that the philosophical base of the right to health as elaborated by the UN and the WHO does indeed have a strong potential to strengthen the right to be fat. But in order to fulfill this potential it is of paramount importance to respect the diversity of human bodies and lifestyles as well as to take the discrimination of fat people seriously.

Introduction

In the late 1990s, fatness was officially declared an epidemic by the World Health Organization (WHO) and other public health organizations and subsequently enormous resources were mobilized to combat the perceived health threat (World Health Organization 2000). More than two decades later, however, public health officials still deplore little progress. Although the scenario of ever-growing waistlines hasn't materialized, at least not in Western countries, there has been no significant reduction in the number of fat people either. And after years of intensive debates on the perils of endemic high body weight the public interest in the issue seems to have calmed down somewhat.

On the other hand, there is increasing attention on the role of nutrition as a major cause of premature deaths. Dietary risks are now described as the number one contributor to avoidable causes of death, even though the risk of premature mortality resulting from nutrition has actually decreased significantly since the 1990s when controlled for age and population growth (GBD Obesity Collaborators 2017). Furthermore, it has been shown time and again that weight does not in fact equate health (Calogero et al. 2019; Flegal 2005; Flegal et al. 2013).

Despite all that, in the public perception and in those of many public health advocates over nutrition and fatness have ousted tobacco consumption as the number one health risk in middle- and high-income countries and increasingly in low-income countries as well. This new focus on food as a public health threat combined with the renewed warnings by public health officials not to underestimate the perils of high body weight have led to a dramatic increase in political measures designed to influence people's diet as well as the size of their bodies (World Health Organization 2015). Due to their asserted severity, the prevention of and the combat against overnutrition and fatness are increasingly presented as part of a right to health (World Health Organization 2017).

Subsequently, I will present the concept of the right to health and the ways it is interpreted in targeting fatness and supposed malnutrition. I will then present two major strains of critique toward these measures. In conclusion, I will suggest an alternative interpretation of the right to health that is consistent with the right to be fat.

The right to health and healthy nutrition

The right to health is defined as a social, cultural, and economic right to a universal standard of health that includes universal access to healthcare and to healthy living conditions. The right to health forms part of several international treaties that were signed and ratified by an overwhelming majority of UN member states. These treaties include but are not limited to the United Nations Human Rights (UNHR) 1948, the United Nations Children's Right Convention (UNCRC) 1990 (not signed by the USA) as well as the International Covenant on Economic, Social and Cultural Rights (ICESR) 1966 (signed, but not ratified by the USA). Another important pillar of the right to health is the concept of Universal Health Coverage that forms part of the United Nations Millennium Development Goals. The principal of Universal Health Coverage is based on the ideal of equity in access to health services as well as the guarantee of quality and affordability of health services (United Nations Department of Public Information 2009; World Health Organization 2004).

The right to health as enshrined in the above-mentioned treaties and conventions was summarized in a fact sheet by the United Nations Commissioner of Human Rights and the World Health Organization in 2008. In this fact sheet the right to health is further explained as an inclusive right that guarantees – among other things – safe drinking water and adequate sanitation, safe food, adequate nutrition and housing, healthy working and environmental conditions, health-related education and information as well as gender equality. It also guarantees freedom from cruel, inhumane or degrading treatment or punishment, and it provides the right to a system of health protections that includes the right to prevention, treatment and control of diseases, access to essential medicines, equal and timely access to basic health services, access to maternal, child and reproductive health, the provision of health-related education and information as well as the participation of the population in health-related decision making. It also states that health services, goods, and facilities must be provided without any discrimination and it guarantees the standard of availability, accessibility, acceptability, and quality of health care products and services for anyone at any given time.

In the above-mentioned fact sheet it is also noted that the right to health is not to be confused with the right to be healthy, since many determinants of health, such as genetics or lifestyle choices, are considered to be rightfully outside the control of the government (Office of the United Nations High Commissioner for Human Rights and World Health Organization 2008).

Although many of the principles of a universal right to health are included in a variety of international agreements and conventions there are relatively few proposals for actual laws that could guarantee the right to health in a given legal system. In order to fill this gap, the World Health Organization (2017) drafted a report on how to reify the right to health in a way that it will have actual meaning in the legal code of countries and thus have real-life consequences for their citizens. This report does not only give general ideas about how public health regulations can be achieved through law reforms, it also looks at ten priorities for public health reform specifically. One of them is dealing with nutrition as well as "overweight and obesity."

Many of the measures that the report proposes with regard to nutrition are already written into law in a growing number of countries. This is especially true for laws concerned with compulsory food labeling as well as for laws demanding food and beverage-related taxes.

Counterarguments against public health laws targeting nutrition and body fat

Although taxes on fat and sugary foods in general and taxes on sugar-sweetened beverages in particular are becoming increasingly popular, the current state of research is inconclusive. There is no consensus on whether sugar-sweetened beverages and weight gain in children and adults are intrinsically linked (Luger et al. 2017). And while studies that investigate the effect of taxes on sugar sweetened beverages in Mexico show a significant decrease in the consumption of these products, they did not show any effect on body weight, therefore complicating the argument of these taxes as being a successful measure against the "obesity-epidemic" (von Philipsborn et al. 2017).

Results are equally inconclusive with regard to the consequences of food labeling in general (Cecchini and Warin 2016; Miller and Cassady 2015) and menu labeling in chain restaurants in particular (Bleich et al. 2017; Cantor et al. 2015). But apart from the question of effectiveness, there is a more general critique concerned with questions of individual freedom, social justice, and human rights. I will describe two different strains of critique toward measures designed to influence people's diet and their body size.

Libertarian argument

The most visible argument against national measures to rein in the eating behaviors and body sizes of their respective citizens derives from a libertarian standpoint. It stresses that food-related health problems should be seen as the sole responsibility of the consumer, as Niko Malek, fellow of the Foundation of Economic Education FEE, one of the oldest neoliberal think tanks in the USA, points out: „The ridiculous claim that corporations are responsible for people's health problems is nothing new. [...]. People who are dying because of smoking-related illnesses have nobody to blame but themselves. And it's the same for people who eat poorly." (Malek 2003) Christopher Snowdon, fellow at the Institute for Economic Affairs IEA, a well established neoliberal think tank in the UK, argues accordingly: „The simple truth is that obesity is, has been, and always will be caused by an excess of calories from any source – frequently also to physical inactivity and various shades of gluttony." (Snowdon 2015a) Following this line of reasoning, any form of governmental intervention deserves critical recognition from this point of view, although measures that inform rather than coerce generally get more leeway than "sin taxes" or outright prohibition of certain foods (Snowdon 2015b). Unsurprisingly, there is a significant overlap with arguments articulated by libertarians and the food industry. But there are also important differences. Rather than trying to make a philosophical argument about personal freedom and liberty, the food industry is framing the issue in terms of nutritional science. The main argument of the food lobby goes like this: there is no such a thing as unhealthy foods, but rather unhealthy lifestyles that may include unhealthy diets. So first of all, the consumption of any given food can be balanced by physical activity, and secondly any given food when consumed in moderate amounts can be part of a healthy diet. Following this rhetorical playbook, the food industry is enacting damage control toward the ever-growing menace of more drastic measures directed at them that are often modeled by established measures against the tobacco industry (Watts et al. 2014). Surprisingly, there is also some overlap between the libertarian argument in favor of governmental restraint, the interests of the food industry, and parts of the food justice movement: for instance regarding the question whether sugar-sweetened beverages should be provided in exchange for food stamps (Hartocollis 2010).

Social justice argument

Public health professionals perceive the fact that people with little financial means are affected more intensely by these so-called sin taxes as beneficiary, because these are the same people who are considered to be the prime consumers of foods and beverages deemed to be unhealthy. Furthermore, fat people are often lower-income (Ernsberger 2009).

The subject is presented as a win-win situation where those who are affected most by additional taxes are also the ones to gain the most (Sassi et al. 2018). In this context, there is little to no recognition of the overwhelming body of evidence that poor living and working conditions, lack of financial stability, high responsibility combined with lack of autonomy and acknowledgment in the workplace and beyond do indeed contribute most to health inequalities, whereas food habits and other consumer choices are seen as a result rather than a cause of poverty (Bambra 2011; Schrecker and Bambra 2015; Wilkinson and Pickett 2010).

Several unintended consequences of higher food taxes are described in the literature. First, people might still consume taxed foods and beverages but switch to lower-quality products in order to compensate for higher prices, or consumers might even cut back on healthy foods to be able to afford their favorite foods (Cornelsen et al. 2014). In this case, sin taxes on certain foods would have the adverse effect by further limiting choice and thereby increasing the reliance of poor people on unhealthy and taxed but still comparably cheap food. This scenario has – at least in part – proven to be the case in Denmark, where a fat tax introduced in 2011 and abolished just 15 months later did little to change consumption patterns, but provoked higher cost for low income consumers who as a result were increasingly looking for cheaper alternatives (Jensen and Smed 2013).

Another more philosophical argument against these interventions is that no matter their effect on the consumption of certain foods, they are paternalizing low-income people, making it harder if not outright impossible (as in the case of the distribution of food stamps) for them to consume certain foods or beverages, thus restraining their individual freedom severely whereas people of higher financial means essentially get a pass. It may well be argued then that one of the pillars of the right to health with regard to nutrition, mainly the right to be "free from hunger and to have an adequate supply of safe and nutritious food" (World Health Organization 2017, 252), could be further imperiled if a growing number of foods are subject to "non-trivial taxes" as recommended by the WHO and the UN.

The right to health and the right to be fat

With that in mind it is worthwhile to take a look at the WHO report "Advancing the right to health and the vital role of law" (2017) more specifically. The report is not only concerned about how to advance the right to health through law reform, it is also setting priorities for concrete public health measures. It identifies ten areas starting with "clean water, sanitation and vector abatement" and ending with "maternal, reproductive and child health". By far the most extensive of these ten priorities is dedicated to legal responses to "poor nutrition, undernutrition, overweight and obesity" (World Health Organization 2017, 251–280).

The section of the report that is dedicated to food-related health problems starts with a reference to the human right to be free from hunger and to have an adequate supply of safe and nutritious food as recognized in the International Covenant on Economic, Social and Cultural Rights (World Health Organization 2017, 252). Nevertheless, the section is rather short on the issue of under- and poor nutrition. The report seems to dismiss the issue of undernutrition as mostly a relic of the past, ignoring the statistics that show that the number of under- and malnourished people worldwide did not see significant reduction since the millennium and did in fact grow again in recent years (Food and Agriculture Organization of the United Nations 2018). Rather, the report claims that the nutritional risks of undernutrition even in many low and middle-income countries are overshadowed by the perils of a Western diet that is actively contributing to the rapid rise of diabetes and other noncommunicable diseases as well as fatness. The report proposes a variety of measures like abolishing subsidies for foods that are deemed to be unhealthy, banning advertisement and promotional techniques to manipulate and shape children's food preferences, banning the vending of certain foods and beverages close to schools and playgrounds, establishing universal food labeling, imposing non-trivial taxes on sugar-sweetened beverages and on foods that are high in salt, saturated fat, and/or added sugar, introducing general sales bans for certain foods, establishing mandatory food standards as well as mandatory standards to improve micronutrients in foods, creating zoning and planning controls as well as incentives for the establishment of stores and stalls selling healthy and fresh food (World Health Organization 2017, 251f.).

The right to health combines both, freedoms and entitlements (cf. Ooms and Hammonds 2018). Freedoms refer to noninterference in a person's private life, whereas entitlements refer to active support. There seems to be a lot of "active support" in the proposed measures to combat fatness and malnutrition, although mostly in the form of restrictions and taxations of certain foods and much less in the form of broadening the access to foods considered to be healthy. What's missing in the report though is the mentioning of freedoms in the form of a right to noninterference in personal food choices and body diversity. The justification for these mostly interventionist measures revolve around the provision in the right to health that guarantees healthy living conditions but it clashes with the concept of respecting genetic diversity as well as individual lifestyles, even if they might not be consistent with societal health goals. What's more, there is indeed a fundamental difference between the latter proposed measures that provide and enable choice like incentives for stores to sell healthy and fresh food in order to deal with "food deserts" in economically depressed areas and restrictions like the proposed exclusion of sugar sweetened beverages in food stamps or "non-trivial taxes" on certain foods that actively hinder and prevent choice (cf. Griffiths and West 2015). Such a distinction is not to be found in the WHO Report where every type of action seems to equally benefit the goal of providing healthy living conditions.

The right to health and the freedom from discrimination

Even more problematic is another aspect of the report: the complete lack of awareness or even any mentioning of weight discrimination and its effect on human health. Theoretically, the right to health as presented in the common report by the Office of the United Nations High Commissioner for Human Rights and the World Health Organization (2008) extensively covers the relation between discrimination and negative health outcomes. Discrimination is defined here as "any form of distinction, exclusion or restriction made on the basis of various grounds which has the effect or purpose of impairing or nullifying the recognition, enjoyment or exercise of human rights and fundamental freedoms. It is linked to the marginalization of specific population groups and it is generally at the root of fundamental structural inequalities in society. This, in turn may make these groups more vulnerable to poverty and ill health." (Office of the United Nations High Commissioner for Human Rights and World Health Organization 2008, 7)

Weight discrimination clearly has the effect of impairing „the enjoyment or exercise of human rights and fundamental freedoms." Furthermore, it is actively marginalizing fat people and thus contributing to structural inequalities in society. There is ample evidence that weight discrimination contributes to poverty, social downward mobility and ill health of fat people through a variety of mechanisms (Ernsberger 2009). Fat hatred leads to fewer economic and career opportunities as well as lower wages (Brunello and D'Hombres 2007; Greve 2008), it negatively affects relationships within families and between intimate partners (Fikkan and Rothblum 2012), it can lead to eating disorders, body image disturbance and other psychological disorders as well as a variety of medical indications such as high cortisol, high cholesterol and overall higher mortality (Almeida, Savoy et al. 2011; Hayward, Vartanian, and Pinkus 2018; Madowitz et al. 2012; Magallares 2012, Pearl, White, and Grilo 2014, Schvey, Puhl, and Brownell 2014, Sutin, Stephan, and Terracciano 2015).

Within healthcare, fat hatred leads to less utilization of health services by fat people and a lower quality of the provided health services for fat people (Drury and Louis 2002). An ever-growing body of literature clearly shows that there is indeed a direct connection between weight-based discrimination, quality of healthcare, availability of healthcare, accessibility and acceptability of healthcare for fat people (Mensinger, Calogero, and Tylka 2016; Teixeira and Budd 2010). The problem seems to be twofold as the quality of healthcare is diminished by lack of sympathy toward and knowledge of special needs of fat people as well as by lack of proper medical equipment to deal with fat people's special needs. Taken together, fat hatred and ignorance actively contribute to the lower overall health status of fat people. Adding to the problem is the fact that repeated attempts to lose weight are not only notoriously ineffective (Gaesser 2009), but also lead to more health problems than a high but stable body weight (Calogero et al. 2019).

Conclusion

Outside of fat studies there is little to no recognition of fat discrimination as an obstacle to the fulfillment of the right to health (Calogero et al. 2019; O'Hara and Gregg 2012; Tirosh 2012). Rather than genuine concern for the negative consequences of weight discrimination there seems to be a renewed fear of a "normalization" of fat bodies among public health professionals. Although there aren't any indications that weight discrimination has diminished – recent studies show just the opposite (Puhl and Liu 2015) – there is a growing concern among some public health professionals that people individually as well as society as a whole could come to terms with their body weight not least because of the work of the fat acceptance movement „which promotes social acceptance of a wide range of body sizes, including extreme obesity" (Burke and Heiland 2018, 221).

Although these authors clearly fear the trend of diminishing weight stigma, they nevertheless do not advocate fat shaming directly. Instead they call for a strategy that "seek[s] to harness peer effects in a positive way to promote and spread healthy behaviors" (Burke and Heiland 2018, 222). But the support for positive peer effect does not seem to suffice in order to achieve general weight loss in the populace. This is shown by the fact that the same special issue of the *Journal of the American Medical Association* that covered the above-cited piece on the "appropriate response on evolving societal norms of obesity" contained several contributions on the advantages of bariatric surgery (Livingston 2018).

This, in return, underlines the fact that from a public health perspective the idea that fat bodies are here to stay rather than being a temporary medical state is still being rejected, despite all the recent attention on weight discrimination by a number of medical organizations (Rubino et al. 2020).

In this context, the social model of disability could help make the case for an inclusive right to health that covers the right to be fat as part of personhood. In

2018 the Secretary-General of the UN issued a report on the rights of persons with disabilities that examined the challenges experienced by persons with disabilities in the enjoyment of their right to health. In this report it was clarified that „having an impairment does not equate to being unhealthy" (United Nations General Assembly 2018, 4). The report goes on to „acknowledge that the notion of impairment varies throughout history, cultures and societies, reflecting the values and norms of a specific time and place. Similarly, many persons with disabilities do not see their bodily and functional diversity as actual impairments, but as positive and normal traits of their identity or as perceived impairments. [...]. Consequently, disability is nowadays understood as a social construct resulting from the interaction between persons with actual or perceived impairments and attitudinal and environmental barriers. Departing from the practice of pity and treatment, persons with disabilities should now be recognized as equal members of a diverse humanity." (United Nations General Assembly 2018, 4)

Following this approach, the right to be fat in order to be consistent with the right to health as proposed by the WHO must not advocate for universal weight loss and it must not punish behavior that is said to – accurately or not – cause weight gain. What it must do instead is to provide for a holistic approach to health that recognizes fat people as „equal members of a diverse humanity." Such an approach to health for all should not only include the protection of discrimination for everyone, it should also support the promotion of social participation and social equality. Because after all: what undoubtedly endangers health more than anything else is social inequality and marginalization.

Disclosure statement

No potential conflict of interest was reported by the author.

ORCID

Friedrich Schorb http://orcid.org/0000-0001-9419-4157

References

Almeida, L., S. Savoy, and P. Boxer. 2011. "The Role of Weight Stigmatization in Cumulative Risk for Binge Eating." *Journal of Clinical Psychology* 67 (3):278–92. doi:10.1002/jclp.20749.

Bambra, C. 2011. *Work, Worklessness, and the Political Economy of Health*. Oxford: Oxford University Press.

Bleich, S. N., C D. Economos, M L. Spiker, K A. Vercammen, E M. VanEpps, J P. Block, B. Elbel, M. Story, and C A. Roberto. 2017. "A Systematic Review of Calorie Labeling and Modified Calorie Labeling Interventions: Impact on Consumer and Restaurant Behavior." *Obesity* 25 (12):2018–44. doi:10.1002/oby.21940.

Brunello, G., and B. D'Hombres. 2007. "Does Body Weight Affect Wages? Evidence from Europe." *Economics and Human Biology* 5 (1):1–19. doi:10.1016/j.ehb.2006.11.002.

Burke, M. A., and F. W. Heiland. 2018. "Evolving Societal Norms of Obesity: What Is the Appropriate Response?" *JAMA* 319 (3):221–22. doi:10.1001/jama.2017.18947.

Calogero, R. M., T L. Tylka, J L. Mensinger, A. Meadows, and S. Daníelsdóttir. 2019. "Recognizing the Fundamental Right to Be Fat: A Weight-Inclusive Approach to Size Acceptance and Healing from Sizeism." *Women & Therapy* 42 (1–2):22–44. doi:10.1080/02703149.2018.1524067.

Cantor, J., A. Torres, C. Abrams, and B. Elbel. 2015. "Five Years Later: Awareness of New York City's Calorie Labels Declined, with No Changes in Calories Purchased." *Health Affairs* 34 (11):1893–900. doi:10.1377/hlthaff.2015.0623.

Cecchini, M., and L. Warin. 2016. "Impact of Food Labelling Systems on Food Choices and Eating Behaviours: A Systematic Review and Meta-analysis of Randomized Studies." *Obesity Reviews* 17 (3):201–10. doi:10.1111/obr.12364.

Cornelsen, L., R. Green, A. Dangour, and R. Smith. 2014. "Why Fat Taxes Won't Make Us Thin." *Journal of Public Health* 37 (1):18–23. doi:10.1093/pubmed/fdu032.

Drury, C. A., and M. Louis. 2002. "Exploring the Association between Body Weight, Stigma of Obesity, and Health Care Avoidance." *Journal of the American Academy of Nurse Practitioners* 14 (12):554–61. doi:10.1111/j.1745-7599.2002.tb00089.x.

Ernsberger, P. 2009. "Does Social Class Explain the Connection between Weight and Health." In *The Fat Studies Reader*, edited by E. Rothblum and S. Solovay, 25–36. New York: New York University Press.

Fikkan, J. L., and E. D. Rothblum. 2012. "Is Fat a Feminist Issue? Exploring the Gendered Nature of Weight Bias." *Sex Roles* 66 (9–10):575–92. doi:10.1007/s11199-011-0022-5.

Flegal, K. M. 2005. "Excess Deaths Associated with Underweight, Overweight, and Obesity." *JAMA: The Journal of the American Medical Association* 293 (15):1861–67. doi:10.1001/jama.293.15.1861.

Flegal, K. M., B K. Kit, H. Orpana, and B I. Graubard. 2013. "Association of All-cause Mortality with Overweight and Obesity Using Standard Body Mass Index Categories: A Systematic Review and Meta-analysis." *JAMA: The Journal of the American Medical Association* 309 (1):71–82. doi:10.1001/jama.2012.113905.

Food and Agriculture Organization of the United Nations [FAO]. 2018. *The State of Food Security and Nutrition in the World 2018: Building Climate Resilience for Food Security and Nutrition*. Rom: Food & Agriculture Org.

Gaesser, G. 2009. "Is "Permanent Weight Loss" an Oxymoron?" In *The Fat Studies Reader*, edited by E. D. Rothblum and S. Solovay, 37–41. New York: New York University Press.

GBD Diet Collaborators. 2017. "Health effects of dietary risks in 195 countries, 1990–2017: A systematic analysis for the Global Burden of Disease Study 2017."*The Lancet* 393 (10184) :1958–1972. doi:10.106/S0140-6736819)/30041-8.

Greve, J. 2008. "Obesity and Labor Market Outcomes in Denmark." *Economics & Human Biology* 6 (3):350–62. doi:10.1016/j.ehb.2008.09.001.

Griffiths, P., and C. West. 2015. "A Balanced Intervention Ladder: Promoting Autonomy through Public Health Action." *Public Health* 129 (8):1092–98. doi:10.1016/j.puhe.2015.08.007.

Hartocollis, A. (2010). "Unlikely Allies in Food Stamp Debate." *New York Times* Accessed October 16, 2010. https://www.nytimes.com/2010/2010/2017/weekinreview/2017hartocollis.html.

Hayward, L. E., L R. Vartanian, and R T. Pinkus. 2018. "Weight Stigma Predicts Poorer Psychological Well-Being through Internalized Weight Bias and Maladaptive Coping Responses." *Obesity (Silver Spring, Md.)* 26 (4):755–61. doi:10.1002/oby.22126.

Jensen, J. D., and S. Smed. 2013. "The Danish Tax on Saturated Fat - Short Run Effects on Consumption, Substitution Patterns and Consumer Prices of Fats." *Food Policy* 42 (1):18–31. doi:10.1016/j.foodpol.2013.06.004.

Livingston, E. H. 2018. "Reimagining Obesity in 2018: A JAMA Theme Issue on Obesity." *Journal of the American Medical Association [JAMA]* 319 (3):238–40. doi:10.1001/jama.2017.21779.

Luger, M., M. Lafontan, M. Bes-Rastrollo, E. Winzer, V. Yumuk, and N. Farpour-Lambert. 2017. "Sugar-sweetened Beverages and Weight Gain in Children and Adults: A Systematic Review from 2013 to 2015 and A Comparison with Previous Studies." *Obesity Facts* 10 (6):674–93. doi:10.1159/000484566.

Madowitz, J., S. Knatz, T. Maginot, S J. Crow, and K N. Boutelle. 2012. "Teasing, Depression and Unhealthy Weight Control Behaviour in Obese Children." *Pediatric Obesity* 7 (6):446–52. doi:10.1111/j.2047-6310.2012.00078.x.

Magallares, A. 2012. "Well-being and Prejudice toward Obese People in Women at Risk to Develop Eating Disorders." *The Spanish Journal of Psychology* 15 (3):1293–302. doi:10.5209/rev_SJOP.2012.v15.n3.39415.

Malek, N. 2003. "Fast Food and Persona Responsibility. Liberty and Responsibility are Inseperable." https://fee.org/articles/fast-food-and-personal-responsibility/

Mensinger, J. L., R M. Calogero, T L. Tylka. 2016. "Internalized Weight Stigma Moderates Eating Behavior Outcomes in Women with High BMI Participating in a Healthy Living Program." *Appetite* 102:32–43. doi:10.1016/j.appet.2016.01.033.

Miller, L. M. S., and D. L. Cassady. 2015. "The Effects of Nutrition Knowledge on Food Label Use. A Review of the Literature." *Appetite* 92: 207–16. doi: 10.1016/j.appet.2015.05.029.

O'Hara, L., and J. Gregg. 2012. "Human Rights Casualties from the "War on Obesity": Why Focusing on Body Weight Is Inconsistent with a Human Rights Approach to Health." *Fat Studies* 1 (1):32–46. doi:10.1080/21604851.2012.627790.

Office of the United Nations High Commissioner for Human Rights and World Health Organization. 2008. The Right to Health Fact Sheet No. 31. Geneva.

Ooms, G., and R. Hammonds. 2018. "The Human Right to Health and Global Health Politics." In *The Oxford Handbook of Global Health Politics*, edited by G. Ooms and R. Hammonds. Oxford. doi:10.1093/oxfordhb/9780190456818.013.30.

Pearl, R. L., M A. White, and C M. Grilo. 2014. "Weight Bias Internalization, Depression, and Self-reported Health among Overweight Binge Eating Disorder Patients." *Obesity (Silver Spring, Md.)* 22 (5):E142–148. doi:10.1002/oby.20617.

Puhl, R. M., and S. Liu. 2015. "A National Survey of Public Views about the Classification of Obesity as A Disease." *Obesity* 23 (6):1288–95. doi:10.1002/oby.21068.

Rubino, F. Rubino, R M. Puhl, D E. Cummings, R H. Eckel, D H. Ryan, J I. Mechanick, J. Nadglowski, X. Ramos Salas, P R. Schauer, et al. 2020. "Joint International Consensus Statement for Ending Stigma of Obesity." *Nature Medicine* 26:485–97. doi:10.1038/s41591-020-0803-x.

Sassi, F., A. Belloni, A J. Mirelman, M. Suhrcke, A. Thomas, N. Salti, S. Vellakkal, C. Visaruthvong, B M. Popkin, and R. Nugent. 2018. "Equity Impacts of Price Policies to Promote Healthy Behaviours." *The Lancet* 391 (10134):2059–70. doi:10.1016/S0140-6736(18)30531-2.

Schrecker, T., and C. Bambra. 2015. *How Politics Makes Us Sick: Neoliberal Epidemics*. New York: palgrave macmillan.

Schvey, N. A., R M. Puhl, and K D. Brownell. 2014. "The Stress of Stigma: Exploring the Effect of Weight Stigma on Cortisol Reactivity." *Psychosomatic Medicine* 76 (2):156–62. doi:10.1097/PSY.0000000000000031.

Snowdon, C. 2015a. "The Ineffectiveness of Food and Soft Drink Taxes." *Cato Unbound. A Journal of Debate*. https://www.cato-unbound.org/2015/01/12/christopher-snowdon/ineffectiveness-food-soft-drink-taxes.

Snowdon, C. 2015b. *Killjoy: A Critique of Paternalism*. London: Institute of Economic Affairs.

Sutin, A. R., Y. Stephan, and A. Terracciano. 2015. "Weight Discrimination and Risk of Mortality." *Psychological Science* 26 (11):1803–11. doi:10.1177/0956797615601103.

Teixeira, M. E., and G. M. Budd. 2010. "Obesity Stigma: A Newly Recognized Barrier to Comprehensive and Effective Type 2 Diabetes Management." *Journal of the American Academy of Nurse Practitioners* 22 (10):527–33. doi:10.1111/j.1745-7599.2010.00551.x.

Tirosh, Y. 2012. "The Right to Be Fat." *Yale Journal of Health Policy, Law, and Ethics* 12 (2):264–335.

United Nations Department of Public Information. 2009. *Millennium Development Goals Report*. New York: United Nations Publications.

United Nations General Assembly. 2018. *Rights of Persons with Disabilities. Note by the Secretary-General*. New York: United Nations Publications.

von Philipsborn, P., et al. 2017. "Adipositas-Prävention: Eine Steuer auf Süßgetränke ist an der Zeit." *Deutsches Ärzteblatt International* 114 (4): A160–A165.

Watts, R. A., S. Heiss, M. Moser, J. Kolodinsky, and R K. Johnson. 2014. "Tobacco Taxes vs Soda Taxes: A Case Study of a Framing Debate in Vermont." *Health Behavior and Policy Review* 1 (3):191–96. doi:10.14485/HBPR.1.3.3.

Wilkinson, R. G., and K. Pickett. 2010. *The Spirit Level: Why Greater Equality Makes Societies Stronger*. New York: Bloomsbury Press.

World Health Organization [WHO]. 2000. Obesity: Preventing and Managing the Global Epidemic: Report of a WHO Consultation. Genf, World Health Organization.

World Health Organization [WHO]. 2004. *Millennium Development Goals*. New Dehli: WHO Regional Office for South-East Asia.

World Health Organization [WHO]. 2015. *Using Price Policies to Promote Healthier Diets*. Kopenhagen: WHO.

World Health Organization [WHO]. 2017. *Advancing the Right to Health: The Vital Role of Law*. Geneva: WHO.

Weight and the law in New Zealand

Cat Pausé and Kathryn Palmer

ABSTRACT
Fat people face discrimination in employment, housing, educational, and healthcare settings; they are vulnerable to the bias and prejudice held against fat people. Yet few places in the world legislate that weight (or physical size) is a protected category under the law. This manuscript reviews the law in New Zealand and considers the options available to fat people in New Zealand who believe they have experienced discrimination because of their fatness. It reflects on whether New Zealand is in breach of international agreements to protect all people from discrimination. An appendix provides a draft Bill that may be submitted in Parliament to amend the existing law and provide equal protection under the law for fat people.

Fat people face discrimination throughout public and private life. They are less likely to be hired, promoted, or paid an equal wage with their colleagues (Caliendo and Lee 2013; Johansson et al. 2009). They are less likely to be supported in education settings (Crandall 1995; Puhl and Heuer 2009), and less likely to receive evidence-based care when they access healthcare (Drury and Louis 2002; Lee and Pausé 2016). Despite the discrimination experienced by fat people, body size is not usually a protected category or status under the law.

In New Zealand, Grey, Pause, and Hales (2018), used the 2018 World Obesity Day to draw attention to fat stigma and call for the government to pass legalization making it illegal to discriminate against fat people. This was not the first time this argument was made in the New Zealand press; Pausé (2016) wrote an Op ed for Fairfax media that began with the assertion, "It is legal to discriminate against me in Aotearoa New Zealand" (para 1). And the media have occasionally reported on weight discrimination issues and the treatment of fatness in employment. These situations usually involved the dismissal or removal of preexisting employees from their current positions within a company due to weight issues. For example, in 2017 dairy company Fonterra removed two fat truck drivers from their driving work as they were heavier than the weight safety limit on the driver's seats (Harris 2017; Iles 2017). Weight discrimination is not a prohibited ground of discrimination under the Human Rights Act in New Zealand even though it occurs frequently and can have negative effects on the ability of those who are fat to gain employment, advance in careers, and seek health advice (Women's Health Action Trust 2013).

There is not an existing literature of scholarly work on fat discrimination within New Zealand. However, there is literature outside of New Zealand and the South Pacific. Kirkland's (2008) work on fatness and legal theory positions weight discrimination within the civil rights context and argues that a logics of personhood is best used to understand what identity categories are recognized as deserving of protection (gender, ability) and which ones (such as weight) are not. Solovay's (2000) book, *Tipping the scales of justice*, remains one of the more exhaustive pieces of scholarship on weight discrimination within the United States. Solovay considers many ways that weight discrimination occurs in the home, education settings, employment, and more. Solovay also addresses the futility of protecting fatness under existing disability legislation, which will be reviewed more fully later. A more global perspective is presented in German legal scholar Stephanie von Liebenstein's (in preparation) chapter in the forthcoming *International handbook of Fat Studies.*

Fat discrimination in New Zealand

Section 21 of the Human Rights Act (1993) (more on this in a moment) does not prohibit discrimination based on weight, physical size, or appearance. And while section 65 of the Human Rights Act covers indirect discrimination, it requires the plaintiff to identify a "prohibited ground of discrimination" listed in section 21, and argue that discrimination based on weight, physical size or appearance has the *effect of* discriminating on that prohibited ground.

The Women's Health Action Trust argued their concerns on weight discrimination, and how it affects women disproportionately, in a revised briefing paper for the Convention on the Elimination of Discrimination Against Women (Parker 2011). They stated that there had been 49 complaints made to the Human Rights Commission between July 2008 and the publication of the paper in 2011 relating to weight discrimination. The majority of these were received from women who experienced mistreatment in pre-employment and employment settings (Parker 2011).

As weight or size is not a prohibited ground of discrimination, there is little formal evidence about the prevalence of such discrimination and complaints made over issues of weight discrimination in New Zealand. According to the Human Rights Commission, occasionally complaints are received about weight discrimination, often related to weight as a safety or appearance issue (M. Leilua, personal communication, August 8, 2018). Even when complaints are made, they are usually made and resolved on a confidential basis; therefore gathering full and accurate statistics on this matter is difficult.

Is New Zealand falling short of its commitment to human rights for fat people?

Human rights act (1993)

In New Zealand, not all bad or unfair treatment is considered discrimination and is prohibited by the law. Further, not all discrimination is unlawful. The Human Rights Act (1993) (Act) has a binding effect in New Zealand law, and sets out the areas where discrimination may be unlawful. These include in employment (both during the application stage and during employment, and applies to all forms of employment, including voluntary work); government services; business partnerships; industrial and professional associations; in access to places, vehicles and facilities; in provision of goods and services; in provision of land or house, and other accommodation; and in education.

Under the Act, the prohibited grounds of discrimination are set out in section 21: these are sex, marital status, religious belief, ethical belief, color, race, ethnic or national origin, disability, age, political opinion, employment status, family status and sexual orientation ("Section 21" 2020). Discrimination based on weight, size or physical appearance is not a prohibited ground of discrimination under section 21.

Section 65 of the Act prohibits indirect discrimination,

> Where any conduct, practice, requirement, or condition that is not apparently in contravention of any provision of this Part has the effect of treating a person or group of persons differently on 1 of the prohibited grounds of discrimination in a situation where such treatment would be unlawful under any provision of this Part other than this section, that conduct, practice, condition, or requirement shall be unlawful under that provision unless the person whose conduct or practice is in issue, or who imposes the condition or requirement, establishes good reason for it ("Section 65" 2020).

Human rights commission

A person who believes they have experienced fat discrimination in New Zealand may file a complaint with the Human Rights Commission (*HRC*) ("How to make a complaint" 2020). The HRC clarifies that the law prohibits discrimination for the prohibited statuses identified in s21 of the Act; although neither weight nor physical size are included in this list, the HRC notes that "You can still contact the HRC if your complaint is about other human rights issues. The enquiries and complaints service can help by providing advice and information, and by suggesting how best to resolve your issue" ("What you can complain about" 2020). If the claim is not resolved following a complaint to the HRC, an individual may file a claim in the Human Rights Review Tribunal (*Tribunal*); the Tribunal hears claims relating to the Act ("Human rights" 2020).

The Tribunal is an independent judicial body that is separate from the HRC and an order from the Tribunal can be enforced the same as any other court order or law. The members are appointed by the Governor-General on the recommendation of the Minister of Justice based on their relevant knowledge of the law, rights, public administration or economic, employment, social or cultural issues. The Tribunal can award up to 350,000 NZD in damages for loss suffered.

The Tribunal operates much like a court, but with more informal aspects to some of its procedure. It is straightforward to file a claim in person, and litigants in the Tribunal may or may not retain legal representation. "Statement of claim" forms are provided on the Tribunal website. The form requires a litigant: to describe the relevant provisions of the Act that are in issue; to describe the facts of the case; and to describe the orders sought from the Tribunal. It is free to file a claim and to appear, but an unsuccessful plaintiff may have costs awarded against them ("Make a claim").

The Tribunal will serve the statement of claim on the defendant(s), who must provide a statement of reply within 30 days of receiving the claim if they intend to defend the claim. The parties then must wait for a teleconference arranged by the Tribunal, at which the Tribunal Chairperson will usually set out a timetable leading up to a hearing. That will include matters like "discovery" (providing any relevant documents to the other side) and filing evidence.

The Tribunal sits as a panel: the Chairperson, Co-Chairperson or Deputy Chairperson is accompanied by two "panel members," who may or may not be legally trained. They will hear the parties' evidence and legal submissions, and deliberate. The Tribunal's hearings are open to the public unless specifically closed (for example, if evidence of a sensitive nature is being given). Decisions are usually provided in writing sometime after the hearing. Decisions of the Tribunal may be appealed to the High Court, and then to the Court of Appeal on a question of law ("Human rights").

As weight discrimination is not currently a prohibited ground of discrimination in New Zealand, it is difficult to predict what the Tribunal might do with a claim that relies on height or weight discrimination. If the claim has some connection to another prohibited ground (for example, race, ethnicity, or disability) the Tribunal might consider it is sufficiently arguable to proceed to a full hearing. A claim with no reasonable connection to a prohibited ground is likely to face difficulties. The Chairperson of the Tribunal may express doubts about the claim at the initial teleconference and the plaintiff may be encouraged to amend or withdraw the claim.

Waitangi Tribunal

Fat Māori (the Indigenous people of Aotearoa New Zealand) may have an additional venue available. The Waitangi Tribunal is a standing commission of inquiry to which individual Māori, or Māori as a collective, can bring complaints relating to legislation policies, actions, or omissions of the Crown that are alleged to breach the principles of the Treaty of Waitangi and its obligations to them under the Treaty of Waitangi. The Treaty of Waitangi is the founding document of New Zealand. A cornerstone of the Treaty is the principle of partnership; it is the overarching tenet from which other principles have been derived. For example, in return for the recognition of governance, the Crown recognizes the principle of tino rangatiratanga – whereby the Crown owes an obligation to actively protect Māori tribal authority, Māori cultural practices, and Māori themselves, as groups and individuals (to learn more about the Treaty of Waitangi, see Human Rights Commission 2010; Te Puni Kokiri/Ministry of Maori Development 2001). Active protection also extends to the principle of equity whereby the Crown is precluded from failing to act (omitting to act) to address inequitable outcomes for Māori under Crown policy.

Theodore, McLean, and TeMorenga (2015) frame the high rates of fatness in Māori as a health disparity that is a breach of the Treaty, citing that "the recognition of Māori rights as indigenous peoples in the Treaty of Waitangi includes the benefits guaranteed to all citizens. This places responsibility on the NZ Government to ensure that Māori have at least the same standard of health as non-Māori" (509). Theodore, McLean, and TeMorenga (2015) argue that fatness in Māori is a direct cause of colonization; pointing to the loss of land, knowledge, and resources experienced by Māori, which combined with poverty, modern obesogenic environments, and racism, create a perfect storm for Māori in New Zealand. Māori, then, could bring a claim about fatness, including the discrimination faced by fat Māori, to the Waitangi Tribunal. Importantly, the Waitangi Tribunal makes non-binding recommendations to the Crown, unlike the Tribunal whose rulings are binding. Therefore, the Tribunal may serve a better avenue for individual Māori seeking to address their experiences with fat discrimination.

Universal declarations

In not providing equal protection under the law for fat people, is New Zealand falling short of its commitment to the global community on human rights' issues? The long title of the Human Rights Act (1993) (Act) recognizes the need to "provide better protection of human rights in New Zealand in general accordance with the United Nations Covenants or Conventions on Human Rights" (9). This long title is not an operative part of the Act but seeks to help guide interpretation of the Act. United Nations Covenants/Conventions are not directly binding in New Zealand, but likewise can be used in domestic courts and tribunals to help guide the interpretation of statutes like the Act. In exploring whether fat people deserve equal protection under the law, there are two United Nations Covenants/Conventions that are particularly relevant.

First, the Universal Declaration of Human Rights (United Nations General Assembly 1948), which New Zealand has ratified, provides 30 articles to be supported and enforced. Of note are Articles 7, "All are equal before the law and are entitled without any discrimination to equal protection of the law" and 2, "Everyone is entitled to all the rights and freedoms set forth in this Declaration, without distinction of any kind, such as race, colour, sex, language, religion, political or other opinion, national or social origin, property, birth, or other status." Weight is a status that falls within "other status," affording fat people entitled to the rights and freedom in the Declaration.

As noted in the introduction of this paper, fat people face discrimination across public settings, including housing, employment, healthcare, and education. As such, they should receive equal protection under the law and the rights and freedoms identified across the Declaration. Additionally, government supported "anti-obesity" policies and a weight-centered health focus can be seen to have contributed to the anti-fat prejudices that result in discrimination against fat bodies (Pausé 2017). In this, the government is failing at more than just providing equal protection under the law for fat people; it is playing an active role in the oppression and discrimination of fat people.

Additionally, New Zealand has endorsed (after originally opposing) the United Nations Declaration on the Rights of Indigenous Peoples (2008). Of note are Articles 21, "Indigenous peoples have the right, without discrimination, to the improvement of their economic and social conditions, including, inter alia, in the areas of education, employment, vocational training and retraining, housing, sanitation, health, and social security," and Article 24, "Indigenous peoples have the right to their traditional medicines and to maintain their health practices ... Indigenous individuals also have the right to access, without any discrimination, to all social and health services. Indigenous individuals have an equal right to the enjoyment of the highest attainable standard of physical and mental health. States shall take the necessary steps with a view to achieving progressively the full realization of this right." These articles speak to the right of Indigenous peoples to lead lives free from discrimination, especially within the public sector. As Māori are more likely to be fat than non- Māori in New Zealand (Ministry of Health 2016), one would expect them to experience greater levels of discrimination because of their size (not to mention the intersection of sizeism and white supremacy they experience).

In short, New Zealand is not living up to its commitment to human rights, as identified by the Universal Declaration of Human Rights and the United Nations Declaration on the Rights of Indigenous Peoples; the lack of anti-discrimination legislation for weight may violate the obligations under these instruments.

Equal protection under the law

Fat people in New Zealand deserve nothing less than equal protection under the law, and yet New Zealand is not alone in its failure to provide equal protection under the law for fat individuals. Worldwide few jurisdictions have anti-discrimination legislation that prohibits discrimination based on weight; those that do include San Francisco and Michigan in the United States, Victoria in Australia, and the city of Reykjavik in Iceland (O'Hara and Gregg 2012). For example, in the state of Michigan in the United States, an amendment was made to the Elliot-Larsen Civil Rights Act of 1976 that prohibited discrimination in employment based on weight. Section 37.2202(1)(a) of the Act has been available to protect people discriminated against based on weight in the years since.

Studies indicate that people in the Global North are supportive of legislation that provides against weight discrimination in employment settings; there is less support for more generalized anti-discrimination legislation (Hilbert et al. 2017; Puhl and Heuer 2011; Puhl, Suh, and Li 2016; Suh et al. 2014). No research has been conducted to assess the New Zealand public's support for legislation to protect against weight discrimination, although a survey of attitudes in Australia found the majority of participants supported legislation prohibiting weight discrimination (Puhl et al. 2015). Puhl, Suh, and Li (2016) report that the support for anti-discrimination from people within the United States has increased over time, and that the greatest support is found in protecting fatness under existing legislation around disabilities.

Disability

The question of fatness as disability has been explored in the Fat Studies literature (see Cooper, 1997; Harjunen 2004; Herndon 2002; Meleo-Erwin 2014; Mollow 2015). Cooper was perhaps the first to ask the question of whether a fat person could be considered disabled; she concluded that she could call herself disabled because of the disabling reality of living in a fat hating culture. Indeed, Solovay (2000) concluded that using disability legislation was an appropriate route for fat people seeking justice. Herndon (2002) argues that the prong of the Americans with Disability Act (ADA) that addresses perceptions of disability provides an avenue for justice for fat people experiencing discrimination. Utilizing the social model of disability, Herndon presents an argument for fat people experiencing barriers in everyday life due to both fat stigma and oppressive built environments. Meleo-Erwin (2014) argues that fat scholars and activists should follow the model of disability justice, and shift away from a politics of inclusion and accommodation to a more radical "dismantling of the social, cultural, and political-economic conditions and structures that create inequality and oppression in the first place" (109). Fat people, though, often reject the label of being disabled, for a multitude of reasons including the conceptualization of disability as being "synonymous with severe physical impairments/limitations," the belief that fatness is mutable, and the further stigmatization they believe it may bestow (Chan and Gillick 2009, 241).

In some Canadian jurisdictions physical size or "obesity" has been successfully argued to be a disability and therefore to fall under a prohibited ground of discrimination (Luther 2010). In Canada this approach has had limited success as the outcome depends on the plaintiff's definition of disability as well as how this is interpreted by the court. In some Canadian jurisdictions the inclusion of a causation requirement for disability means that cases of alleged weight discrimination have not been successful. Cases that have succeeded have usually done so due to the employer perceiving the plaintiff's weight as a disability rather than the plaintiff proving their weight was an actual disability (Luther 2010). The focus on perceived disability fails to capture the reasons behind discrimination as well as only capturing those who can connect weight to a perceived disability and not those who are of a weight slightly higher than society's perceived ideal (Luther 2010).

It has been suggested, although not yet tested in court, that a similar argument could be made in New Zealand under this ground too (Sneyd 2013). We believe that existing disability legislation is open as an avenue for fat people seeking recourse from weight discrimination. And we agree with scholars (such as Cooper and Herndon) who argue that living life as a fat person in oppressive built environments is debilitating. But receiving equal protection under the disability legislation would be at the whim of the court in each individual case, and this is simply not good enough.

To conclude

As seen in the earlier example from Fonterra, the fat drivers were discriminated against by both the built environment (the seat) and the perception of their employer (that they were unable to continue the job due to their size). In this case, the two workers were offered a "health and wellness" program if they wished to continue driving, or other roles within the company if the remained at their current size (Iles 2017). While it was beneficial that these two workers did not lose their job, the perception by the employer that they could simply lose weight if they desired to remain in their roles is rooted in anti-fat attitudes and oppression. And nothing was suggested that the seats could be adjusted or purposefully built to accommodate a wider range of body sizes.

A better way for justice for fat people is equal protection under the law based on their fatness And not on the conditions of a fat-hating society resulting in their disablement. To provide equal protection under the law for fat people, the government needs to amend the Human Rights Act (1993) to add physical size (meaning weight, height, shape) to the list of protected grounds.

New Zealand should take the required steps to become the first country to provide equal protection under the law for fat people. To encourage the government to take this step, the Appendix of this article includes the text of a possible Bill that could be introduced in Parliament today.

Acknowledgments

Thank you to Tania Te Whenua and Greg Robins for their assistance in understanding the legal system in Aotearoa New Zealand; any misrepresentations in the manuscript are ours.

Disclosure statement

No potential conflict of interest was reported by the authors.

ORCID

Cat Pausé http://orcid.org/0000-0003-1812-6632

References

Caliendo, M., and W. S. Lee. 2013. "Fat Chance! Obesity and the Transition from Unemployment to Employment." *Economics & Human Biology* 11 (2):121–33. doi:10.1016/j.ehb.2012.02.002.

Chan, N. K. C., and A. C. Gillick. 2009. "Fatness as a Disability: Questions of Personal and Group Identity." *Disability & Society* 24 (2):231–43. doi:10.1080/09687590802652520.

Cooper, C. 1997. "Can a Fat Woman Call Herself Disabled?" *Disability & Society* 12 (1):31–42. doi:10.1080/09687599727443.

Crandall, C. S. 1995. "Do Parents Discriminate against Their Heavyweight Daughters?" *Personality and Social Psychology Bulletin* 21 (7):724–35. doi:10.1177/0146167295217007.

Drury, C. A., and M. Louis. 2002. "Exploring the Association between Body Weight, Stigma of Obesity, and Health Care Avoidance." *Journal of the American Academy of Nurse Practitioners* 14 (12):554–61. doi:10.1111/j.1745-7599.2002.tb00089.x.

Grey, L., C. Pause, and I. Hales. October 11, 2018. "Researchers Call for End to Fat Stigma. Press Release." *University of Otago*. https://www.otago.ac.nz/news/news/otago697577.html .

Harjunen, H. 2004. "Exploring Obesity through the Social Model of Disability." In *Gender and Disability Research in the Nordic Countries*, edited by T. Rannveig and K. Kristiansen, 305–24. Lund: Studentlitteratur.

Harris, C. August 30, 2017. "Overweight Driver Standowns at Fonterra a Bigger Industry Issue – Experts." *Stuff* [Online]. https://www.stuff.co.nz/business/industries/96308178/overweight-driver-standowns-at-fonterra-a-bigger-industry-issue–experts .

Herndon, A. 2002. "Disparate but Disabled: Fat Embodiment and Disability Studies." *National Women's Studies Association Journal* 14 (3):120–37.

Hilbert, A., C. Hübner, G. Schmutzer, S. Danielsdottir, E. Brähler, and R. Puhl. 2017. "Public Support for Weight-related Antidiscrimination Laws and Policies." *Obesity Facts* 10 (2):101–11. doi:10.1159/000456012.

"How to make a complaint". 2020. "Human Rights Commission." https://www.hrc.co.nz/enquiries-and-complaints/how-make-complaint/ .

Human Rights Act. 1993. http://www.legislation.govt.nz/act/public/1993/0082/latest/whole.html#DLM304475 .

Human Rights Commission. 2010. "Human Rights and the Treaty of Waitangi." In *Human Rights in New Zealand*, 38–54. Wellington: Author.

"Human rights". 2020. "Human Rights Tribunal." https://www.justice.govt.nz/tribunals/human-rights/ .

Iles, J. August 29, 2017. "Fonterra Truck Drivers Stood down over Weight Concerns." *Stuff* [Online]. https://www.stuff.co.nz/business/96291986/fonterra-truck-drivers-stood-down-over-weight-concerns?rm=m .

Johansson, E., P. Böckerman, U. Kiiskinen, and M. Heliövaara. 2009. "Obesity and Labour Market Success in Finland: The Difference between Having a High BMI and Being Fat." *Economics & Human Biology* 7 (1):36–45. doi:10.1016/j.ehb.2009.01.008.

Kirkland, A. 2008. *Fat Rights: Dilemmas of Difference and Personhood.* New York: NYU Press.

Lee, J. A., and C. J. Pausé. 2016. "Stigma in Practice: Barriers to Health for Fat Women." *Frontiers in Psychology* 7:2063. doi:10.3389/fpsyg.2016.02063.

Luther, E. 2010. "Justice for All Shapes and Sizes: Combatting Weight Discrimination in Canada." *Alberta Law Review* 48 (1):167–88. doi:10.29173/alr167.

"Make a claim". 2020. "Human Rights Tribunal." https://www.justice.govt.nz/tribunals/human-rights/make-a-claim/ .

Meleo-Erwin, Z. 2014. "Queering the Linkages and Divergences: The Relationship between Fatness and Disability and the Hope for a Livable World." In *Queering Fat Embodiment*, edited by C. Pausé, J. Wykes, and S. Murray, 97–114. Surrey: Ashgate.

Ministry of Health. 2016. *Annual Update of Key Results 2015/16: New Zealand Health Survey.* Wellington: Ministry of Health.

Mollow, A. 2015. "Disability Studies Gets Fat." *Hypatia: A Feminist Journal of Philosophy* 30 (1):199–216. doi:10.1111/hypa.12126.

O'Hara, L., and J. Gregg. 2012. "Human Rights Casualties from the "War on Obesity": Why Focusing on Body Weight Is Inconsistent with a Human Rights Approach to Health." *Fat Studies* 1 (1):32–46. doi:10.1080/21604851.2012.627790.

Parker, G. 2011. "CEDW NGO Perspectives." Revised Briefing Paper, Women's Health Action. https://www.womens-health.org.nz/wp-content/uploads/2014/08/Pacific-Womens-Watch-NZ_CEDAW-NGO-Report_Sept-2011_Appendix-2_Health1.pdf .

Pausé, C. J. March 18, 2016. "Being Fat in New Zealand." *Stuff* [Online]. https://www.stuff.co.nz/life-style/life/78052099/opinion-being-fat-in-new-zealand .

Pausé, C. J. 2017. "Borderline: The Ethics of Fat Stigma in Public Health." *The Journal of Law, Medicine & Ethics* 45 (4):510–17. doi:10.1177/1073110517750585.

Puhl, R. M., and C. A. Heuer. 2009. "The Stigma of Obesity: A Review and Update." *Obesity* 17 (5):941–64. doi:10.1038/oby.2008.636.

Puhl, R. M., and C. A. Heuer. 2011. "Public Opinion about Laws to Prohibit Weight Discrimination in the United States." *Obesity (Silver Spring)* 19:74–82. doi:10.1038/oby.2010.126.

Puhl, R. M., J. D. Latner, K. S. O'Brien, J. Luedicke, S. Danielsdottir, and X. R. Salas. 2015. "Potential Policies and Laws to Prohibit Weight Discrimination: Public Views from 4 Countries." *The Milbank Quarterly* 93 (4):691–731. doi:10.1111/1468-0009.12162.

Puhl, R. M., Y. Suh, and X. Li. 2016. "Legislating for Weight-based Equality: National Trends in Public Support for Laws to Protect Weight Discrimination." *International Journal of Obesity* 40:1320–24. doi:10.1038/ijo.2016.49.

"Section 21". 2020. "Human Rights Act 1993." *Section 21.* http://www.legislation.govt.nz/act/public/1993/0082/latest/DLM304475.html .

"Section 65". 2020. "Human Rights Act 1993." *Section 65.* http://www.legislation.govt.nz/act/public/1993/0082/latest/DLM304657.html .

Sneyd, R. April 17, 2013. "Could Employees Claim Discrimination Based on Their Weight?" *Human Resources Director* [Online]. https://www.hrmonline.co.nz/news/could-employees-claim-discrimination-based-on-their-weight-174434.aspx .

Solovay, S. 2000. *Tipping the Scales of Justice.* Amherst, NY: Prometheus Books.

Suh, Y., R. M. Puhl, S. Liu, and F. F. Milici. 2014. "Support for Laws to Prohibit Weight Discrimination in the United States: Public Attitudes from 2011 to 2013." *Obesity (Silver Spring)* 22:1872–79. doi:10.1002/oby.20750.

Te Puni Kokiri/Ministry of Maori Development. 2001. *He Tirohanga O Kawa Ki Te Tiriti O Waitangi: A Guide to the Principles of the Treaty of Waitangi as Expressed by the Courts and the Waitangi Tribunal.* Wellington: Author.

Theodore, R., R. McLean, and L. TeMorenga. 2015. "Challenges to Addressing Obesity for Māori in Aotearoa/New Zealand." *Australian and New Zealand Journal of Public Health* 39 (6):509–12. doi:10.1111/1753-6405.12418.

United Nations General Assembly. 1948. "Universal Declaration of Human Rights." http://www.un.org/en/universal-declaration-human-rights/ .

United Nations General Assembly. 2008. "United Nations Declaration on the Rights of Indigenous Peoples." www.un.org/esa/socdev/unpfii/documents/DRIPS_en.pdf

Von Liebenstein, S. in preparation. "Fatness, Discrimination & Law: An International Perspective." In *International Handbook of Fat Studies*, edited by C. Pause and S. R. Taylor. London: Routledge.

"What you can complain about". 2020. "Human Rights Commission." https://www.hrc.co.nz/enquiries-and-complaints/what-you-can-complain-about/ .

Women's Health Action Trust. 2013. "Universal Periodic Review Submission on the Right to Health - Improving the Health of Women in Aotearoa New Zealand." https://www.hrc.co.nz/files/5714/2406/3062/UPR-submission-Improving-womens-health-in-New-Zealand-2.docx.

Appendix A. Draft bill

Human Rights Act 1993 Amendment Bill

Explanatory Note
General Policy Statement

Under current legislation, fat people can be legally discriminated against. This Bill aims to correct this by introducing physical size, understood as weight, height, and/or shape, as a prohibited ground of discrimination in section 21 of the Human Rights Act (1993).

Clause by clause analysis

Clause 1 is the title clause.

Clause 2 is the commencement clause. It provides for the Bill to come into force on the day after the date on which it receives the Royal assent.

Clause 3 provides that the Bill amends the Human Rights Act (1993) (the **Principal Act**).

Clause 4 amends Section 21 (1) of the principal Act in order to include physical size as a prohibited grounds of discrimination.

Contents

1 Title
This Act is the Human Rights Amendment Act 2018.

2 Commencement
This Act comes into force on the day after the date on which is receives the Royal assent.

3 Principal Act
This Act amends the Human Rights Act 1993 (the Principal Act).

4 Section 21 amended 1
After Section 21 (1) (m), insert:
(n) physical size, which means weight, height, or shape of the body.

Index

For Product Safety Concerns and Information please contact our EU
representative GPSR@taylorandfrancis.com
Taylor & Francis Verlag GmbH, Kaufingerstraße 24, 80331 München, Germany

www.ingramcontent.com/pod-product-compliance
Ingram Content Group UK Ltd.
Pitfield, Milton Keynes, MK11 3LW, UK
UKHW050055200926
475702UK00019B/2842
9781032230375